DO GOOD *At* WORK

"This is a rare book about making work meaningful that's both actionable and fun to read."

—Adam Grant, *New York Times* bestselling author of *Give and Take* and *Originals* and host of the TED podcast WorkLife

"*Do Good At Work* is both a riveting and vital read for corporate leaders, especially now. The events of 2020 have demonstrated that companies need to play an increasingly larger role in the broader society. Bea Boccalandro guides us to this future. Using engaging writing and sound research, she shows us that it's possible to infuse every employee's work with purpose in a way that benefits society, employees and the business. *Do Good At Work* is transformative: It turns its readers into inspired leaders."

—Jan Jones Blackhurst, member of the Caesars Entertainment Board of Directors and former Mayor of Las Vegas

"I would put *Do Good At Work* as among the best business books ever—for both managers and non-managers. It's inspiring yet practical, eye-opening yet digestible and soundly researched yet deeply engaging. Its advice is so practical one wonders why it has taken so long for the word to get out."

—Cynthia Currin, Vice President at JBS International

"As a professor and organizational/leadership development consultant, I have learned that to be a great, agile and future-ready organization or leader, we must be focused on lifting with purpose. We must do good at work. There is no better person to deliver this message than Bea Boccalandro. *Do Good At Work* should be on every leader's shortlist of books to read this year. I am excited for all of the good that will come to this world because of it."

—Ryan Gottfredson, author of *Wall Street Journal* and *USA Today* national bestseller *Success Mindsets*

"Do Good At Work is a wonderful read that will inspire frontline workers, managers and leaders to enhance the work environment to create higher purpose and effect positive outcomes. In turn, this will provide value to employees, owners and communities—a win-win-win strategy. The author uses both quantitative research results and memorable anecdotes to make a compelling case for why we should all work to evolve and transform the workplace."

—Tom Mutryn, CFO of CACI International and former CFO of US Airways

"I LOVED *Do Good At Work*! Its insightful writing provides compelling stories and characters throughout the book that drive home the impactful message that our jobs can provide us with more than just an income; they can provide us with a sense of purpose. Interesting, funny, and engaging, it is also packed with data-driven evidence and strategies to help workers at any level within their organization make their work more meaningful. I encourage everyone to pick up this book and make the investment in themselves; you'll be immensely glad you did."

—Chris Lacey, Founder and President of Autism ALERT, Inc.

DO
GOD
At
WORK

*How Simple Acts
of Social Purpose
Drive Success
and Wellbeing*

Bea Boccalandro

NEW YORK

LONDON • NASHVILLE • MELBOURNE • VANCOUVER

DO GOOD *At* WORK
How Simple Acts of Social Purpose Drive Success and Wellbeing

Published in New York, New York, by Morgan James Publishing. Morgan James is a trademark of Morgan James, LLC. www.MorganJamesPublishing.com

ISBN 978-1-64279-752-7 paperback
ISBN 978-1-64279-753-4 eBook
Library of Congress Control Number: 2019911846

Cover Design by:
Rachel Lopez
www.r2cdesign.com

Illustrations by:
Bea Boccalandro

Morgan James is a proud partner of Habitat for Humanity Peninsula and Greater Williamsburg. Partners in building since 2006.

Get involved today! Visit
www.MorganJamesBuilds.com

For Raul

TABLE OF CONTENTS

I. FLOUNDERING:
WHY WORK FAILS US

Chapter 1

PUTTING A FINGER ON
THE BEST PART OF WORK

"Want to know the best part of work?"

I nod vigorously.

The civil engineer hitches his khaki pants up over his belly and walks past a wall of framed diplomas to a blueprint taped to the wall. He places his nicotine-stained index finger on a small symbol. I run across the room and put my face up against the paper but learn nothing. My father, Tony Boccalandro, seems to be pointing at a complicated letter that I've yet to learn.

My dad manages a team of road engineers for the Venezuelan Ministry of Transportation. His current charge is to eliminate the chronic traffic created by Caracas' international airport. The airport sits on a narrow strip of land between the Caribbean Sea and a formidable mountain with slums at its base. His finger rests on the "best part" of his recent labor.

"Papi, what is it?" I ask. I'm fascinated by work because it's as irresistible to my dad as horseback riding is to me. I can't wait to find out why. Applying my six-year-old logic, I conclude that the "best part" of this mysterious thing called work must be even more fun than my greatest joy: gliding weightlessly atop a galloping horse.

Papi moves his finger to his lips, suppresses a smile and whispers, "Shhh. It's something wonderful that we snuck in without asking permission!"

Now I'm desperate to know what the unauthorized best part of work is. "Papi, what is it?" I screech.

"It's a room to lock up little girls with big brown eyes who ask their poor father the same question over and over," he teases.

"Is it a stable for horses?" I ask

He shakes his head.

"Paaaaapi, what is it?"

He clears his throat with dramatic flair and declares, "It's a footbridge to the beach!"

I frown. This doesn't seem like a great thing. "Why do we need a bridge?" I ask.

"Oh, sweetie, it's not for us," Papi says. He explains that the bridge gives families who live in the adjacent slum access to the beach. Because it's daunting and dangerous to cross four lanes of speeding vehicles, most of these impoverished residents haven't wet their feet in the blue water they see from their homes. "Imagine families who have never played in the sand or splashed in the waves doing just that!" exclaims my beaming father.

I think he expects me to clap. Instead, I pout and cross my arms. "I thought it was something fun, like a horse I could ride." My father walks across the room, rolls his swivel chair back to where I stand, sits down, looks straight into my eyes and holds both of my hands.

Papi uses his most tender nickname for me, which translates to "my precious little sky." He says, "*Mi cielito lindo*, you will need to find better sources of joy as you grow up. You will need to…" He clears his throat before he concludes with, "Listen beyond the clamor of your wants for the whisper of the world's needs."[1]

Listen beyond the clamor of your wants for the whisper of the world's needs.

-Papi

The Tantalizing Possibility of Doing Good at Work

My dad's work beckoned him like a beloved hobby, infused his days with meaning and brought him enduring joy. This book is your manual to making your own work equally fulfilling, regardless of your profession. If you already revel in work that feels great, this book will help ensure that you still do in one year, ten years and on the day you retire.

Over the last twenty years, I have explored the practice my father embodied and urged me toward: doing good at work. It's a scintillating concept. If our daily labor meaningfully contributed to others or to societal causes, had what is known as "social purpose," the world would certainly be more just, kind and pristine. Some professions, including healthcare and firefighting, inherently promote social purpose. But could they do more? What about jobs that don't intrinsically contribute to societal causes? For example, what about driving a truck filled with commercial goods, parking cars at a garage, managing a plant that manufactures industrial chemicals, working from home for a professional services company, serving as an administrative assistant to the marketing director at a bank or running the front office at a storage facility? Is trying to do good from such capitalistic jobs feasible? It is. I'll share how workers in each of these jobs made their workday matter.

My team and I have helped companies build their versions of Papi's pedestrian bridge, including Aetna, Bank of America, DPR Construction, Eventbrite, FedEx, HP, IBM, PwC, QVC, TOMS Shoes, Toyota and Western Digital. Workers ranging from retail clerks to senior executives across the world have made customer interactions more human, products more inclusive, meetings more meaningful, operations more environmentally sustainable, marketing more charitable and otherwise tilted toward good whatever part of work they control. I've also instructed hundreds of Georgetown University mid-career students and thousands of audience members on using work as a platform for meaningful contributions.

All along, we've tracked how those who do good at work fare. We've surveyed tens of thousands and interviewed hundreds of workers and their managers to determine what effect workplace social purpose has on them. We've conducted formal research in Europe, Latin America and the United States on the relationship between doing good at work and work motivation, satisfaction, retention, engagement, performance and other indicators of success and wellbeing. Thankfully, I'm not the only nerd drawn to this topic. Management professors and other business experts have also studied and measured the impact of doing good at work. Furthermore, dozens of biologists, economists, organizational behaviorists, physicians, psychologists, neuroscientists and other specialists have studied the psychological, health, career and life effects of doing good at work.

What we've learned is exhilarating. No matter who we are or what our job is, we can do work that matters. We can end our workweek delighted to have lightened the burden of an exhausted single mother, given an injured soldier hope, brought a smile to an autistic child, helped polar bears avoid extinction or otherwise brightened some recess of the planet.

Whether our workplace is an assembly line, office, tractor-trailer or our home, doing good at work is not only feasible—it's our birthright. Anthropologists now know that prehistoric humans worked not for their own families, but for the collective. They hunted woolly mammoths not for their family's icebox, but for a tribal feast. They cleared trees not to build their own hut, but to raise the entire village.

When a pandemic, disaster, divorce or other crisis halts our habitual hustle and elicits reflection, many of us sense that our work is meant to be similarly grand. When our neighbors are wheeled into hospitals or lose their jobs, we feel inadequate merely selling luxury goods, planning a budget meeting or otherwise doing the narrowly conceived job we performed semi-automatically days earlier. This discomfort is our evolutionary legacy bubbling up to our modern consciousness. Thousands of generations of ancestors bestowed on us an instinctual longing, innate ability and great joy in performing work that has social purpose.

We are so hardwired to make work-based contributions to society that it's actually good for us. Dozens of studies provide overwhelming evidence that social purpose boosts our work motivation, productivity, satisfaction and performance. Work with social purpose also makes it less likely that our Mondays feel dreadful, that we wake up at 3:00 a.m. stricken by fear, that we get sick or that we end up feeling alone and forgotten. Instead, we are more likely to face life's challenges calmly, enjoy happiness, stay healthy and live longer.

Sure, it takes a tad of rebellion and a dash of creativity to sneak a pedestrian bridge for impoverished families into a blueprint or otherwise extend the boundaries of our jobs to do good. But that's only because the modern workplace, with its sterile culture and rigid professionalism, has become an aberration of human habitat. Yet, we know it's possible to shape contemporary labor toward social purpose. Many people already have, including my father and the workers at the six jobs mentioned above. The practice of doing good at work is not exotic, new-age or all that innovative. It's surprisingly natural and intuitive—once we remove a few barriers. Doing good at work is how we get beyond bringing only a fractured version of ourselves to work. It's how we banish the chronic ache of our unmet longing for meaningful work. Infusing our work with social purpose is nothing less than a path to restoring the whole of who we are.

This book distills decades of my work, scores of research studies from across the world and the experience of thousands of workplace social-purpose pioneers into concrete lessons on how to ignite a sense of purpose at work. Its overarching message is this: Any of us can catapult our success and wellbeing by doing good at work.[2] Ready to start?

Unhappy Work, Unhappy Life

Why do I help people make their work life fulfilling? After all, doesn't fulfillment come from our personal lives? Aren't I overvaluing work? I get these questions in boardrooms, auditoriums and across the dinner table. Many of us have been socialized to believe that work is merely a mechanism to afford the stuff that brings us joy. Research, however, has reached the opposite conclusion. Whether we like it or not, work directly impacts our happiness.

I baked a quiche for a dinner party once. Its flavor was allegedly mushroom cheddar, but it tasted more like flavorless gelatin. I tried to highlight the crisp green salad during dinner conversation, but a side dish couldn't redeem the meal. Many of us make this same mistake with work. If our jobs aren't fulfilling, we resort to the popular practice of work-life balance. We try to counter work's blandness with golf, movies or volunteering during the waking hours that work does not occupy. These are worthy things to do, but they are the side dishes that can't make up for a bland main course. Typically, evening and weekend activities can't pull us out of work-caused doldrums.

Work and life are so interwoven that if our job satisfaction drops by 10 percent, our life satisfaction drops, on average, by 6 percent.[3] According to a Gallup study, if we're dissatisfied with work, it's likely (68 percent probability) that we're not highly satisfied with life and, conversely, if we are satisfied with work, it's likely (79 percent probability) that we are highly satisfied with life.[4] Similarly, another survey found that for those of us who work fulltime, it's almost impossible to feel fulfilled in life if we don't feel fulfilled at work. The chances are one in 100.[5]

Qualitative research corroborates the tenacious link between job satisfaction and life satisfaction. University of Illinois professor Archie Green dedicated his lifetime listening to songs, reciting poems and reading novels related to labor. He found that the modern folklore of work reveals that our fundamental, albeit often subconscious, belief is, "I work, therefore I am."[6]

Consider how we speak to new acquaintances. "What's your work?" is often an early inquiry. It's not just small talk. We view and treat a

I work, therefore I am.

-Archie Green

drummer differently than a dentist, even if their physiques, hometowns, attire, personalities and other attributes are identical. Our image of someone we meet at a bar is colored by whatever labor they did earlier that day.

Indeed, our ancestors thought work was central enough to personal identity that they named each other by it. The most common last name in the English-speaking world, Smith, refers to a blacksmith or metalsmith. If your surname is Archer, Brewer, Chamberlain, Fisher, Fletcher, Harper, Mason, Miller or Turner, you have an ancestor who was named for a job. This naming convention is not just a quirk of work-obsessed Anglo-Saxons. One of the most common Chinese surnames, Zhang, means bowmaker and the popular Indian surname, Gandhi, means perfume seller. Today our last names might be set, but we add "Senator," "General" and "Doctor" to them. Similarly, lawyers adorn their names with "Esq," accountants with "CPA" and project managers with "PMP." Whether consciously or subconsciously, we consider work so central to our sense of self that we use it to shape our names—the very symbols that represent us.

Jobs affect us so profoundly that losing them often precipitates feelings of worthlessness beyond what the associated financial hardship can explain.[7] That is, our labor is a pillar of our sense of self. Of course, work's profound effect would be fine if it shaped us into happy beings. But it usually doesn't. Twentieth-century journalist Studs Terkel interviewed hundreds of people about their work and concluded that, for many, it felt like a "Monday-through-Friday sort of dying."[8] Does recent data confirm this sobering assessment?

There is no research comparing how much we enjoy being dead as opposed to being at work. One study, however, comes close. U.K. researchers studied whether we prefer working to being sick in bed, arguably the closest we can come to death and still participate in the study. Guess what? There's not much difference. Being sick in bed brings us the least amount of joy out of thirty-nine typical daily activities. Work, however, is barely better, ranking thirty-eighth.[9] We would rather scrub the tub or get stuck in traffic than work on the boss' project.

The above study is on U.K. workers, but there is ample evidence that work dissatisfaction is a global phenomenon. Gallup measures levels of U.S. work satisfaction every year. In no year during the 21st century have more than 55 percent of Americans been satisfied with their jobs.[10] On average, only 47 percent have. A different study found that 46 percent of Americans are largely dissatisfied with their jobs.[11] Furthermore, a survey of 18,000 workers in fifty-six countries found that only 28 percent consider their work experience positive.[12]

To be clear, I've turned down speaking engagements because they conflicted with my mom's birthday, the opportunity to hike with friends and my unwillingness to deliver a speech after an overnight flight. I confer more importance on my personal life than on doing more work. Surveys find that most of us do.[13] Nevertheless, work defines our lives in the same way an entrée defines a meal. If work is unsatisfying, it's likely our life is as well. And, unfortunately, work often is unsatisfying. For many of us, our labor obstructs our chance of happiness. It doesn't have to be this way.

We Can Make Work and Life Fulfilling

No matter what our job is, we can end our workday uplifted by the knowledge that we made a difference in the world. The first step, however, is to understand and stop doing what we're doing wrong. For that lesson, we are going to travel in time to the 1990s when I was in my twenties.

Chapter 2

PUTTING MONEY IN ITS PLACE

I 'm at my home office, which consists of a desk wedged into the den's back corner. My shoulders droop and my eyes glaze over as I try to focus on the computer screen. My husband, Dirk, twirls my chair, wraps his arms around me and whispers my pet name.

"Just quit," he says.

"That's ridiculous," I think. I'm analyzing data. I know this sounds dull to most people, but I tilt toward geek. The prospect of running statistics on a database lures me to my computer first thing every morning, half-eaten bagel in hand. On most days, I'm blissfully absorbed in a sea of numbers before I take my last bite.

Until recently, anyway.

Mysterious Demotivation

Over the last six months, work has gone from feeling like a game that's hard to stop playing to a duty that's hard to continue performing. I don't know why. I'm happy with my salary and learning continually. My coworkers make me laugh often and pull my hair out only occasionally. My boss, Jo Ann, is visionary and supportive. Once after several weeks of intense work, she shooed me out of the office and into my weekend on a Thursday morning. As I walked out, she handed me tickets to a Neil Young concert. If anything, I should cherish this job. The idea of quitting is absurd.

Three weeks later, I walk into Jo Ann's office.

"I need to quit," I state.

Jo Ann responds, "We can raise your pay."

"That's not it," I say.

"We can assign Josh to someone else," she answers. (Josh was an unpleasant client and, no, that's not his real name.)

An awkward silence ensues. Seated on Jo Ann's tan sofa, I'm staring at my jittery left foot as if it needed intense supervision.

Jo Ann asks, "Do you want a more challenging project?"

"Uh, I don't think so," I say. There's another awkward silence. I shift my gaze to my right shoe. After a few seconds, I finally look up.

From the way Jo Ann tilts her head and tightens her lips, I can practically see a thought bubble above her head. It reads, "Hmm, Bea is mildly deranged."

I agree. If I were sane, I would accept the raise and feel happier about my decent job. Jo Ann knows this. I know this. Most people know this. Instead, I choose unemployment and its associated emotional and economic distress.

Not to blame Dirk for my wacky decision, but he convinced me to walk away from that job. I expressed several valid objections to his suggestion that I quit. "We need the money…I'm treated well…It's a decent job…Maybe I'm expecting too much from work…I must be the problem."

Dirk's response to each was the same: "You are too wonderful for lame work." It was a sweet and supportive retort. But was it good advice?

The Limitations of Money

It turns out that dismissing Jo Ann's raise as a remedy for my malaise was not a sign of derangement. Thanks to a sharp turn in our understanding of human motivation, my questionable 1990s decision now sits under the banner of perfectly logical behavior.

For most of the twentieth century, economists asserted that pay, perks and other tangible benefits—known as "extrinsic rewards"—motivated our work and boosted our job satisfaction. Toward the end of the century, however, psychologist Daniel Kahneman started empirically testing this contention and inspired others to do the same. Their findings were so revelatory that they resulted in Kahneman, a non-economist, earning the 2002 Nobel Prize in Economics. Kahneman and followers debunked what economists and most people had considered irrefutable. They disproved that pay and other extrinsic rewards increase job satisfaction and motivation.

A Harvard Business School study offered an hourly wage that was 33 percent higher to a random subset of online workers. Higher pay had no effect on their productivity. It did not motivate them to perform any better than the lower-paid control group.[14] There is also evidence that pay largely fails to improve how satisfying our work is. A systematic review of over ninety studies concluded that 85 percent of our job satisfaction has nothing to do with pay.[15] Put another way, all the pay in the world corresponds with an increase in job satisfaction of no more than 15 percent.

It appears that Jo Ann's raise would have changed nothing for me. Within months of receiving higher pay, I would have struggled with my motivation and complained about my job as much as ever. I'm not basing this statement on the few studies mentioned above. In conducting research for this book, I printed all the research from the last thirty years concluding that monetary and other extrinsic rewards don't improve job motivation or satisfaction. I became the overwhelmed owner of a leaning tower of paper about a foot tall. The pile had the above-mentioned research reports plus studies on dental, manufacturing, military, office, service, university and other types of jobs. It included studies on workers in Australia, Bangladesh, India, Nigeria, Taiwan, the United Kingdom, the United States and other countries.

To be fair, I also uncovered studies showing that extrinsic rewards boosted job motivation and satisfaction.[16] These printouts, however, stood a mere inch tall. So, yes, money can motivate under certain conditions. First, pay can motivate if the task we are doing is rudimentary, repetitive, manual and requires close to no thinking. If our job is stuffing envelopes or placing labels on jars in an assembly line, monetary incentives might push us into high gear month after month. Second, if we need financial resources for our survival or safety, or that of our family, money might motivate us. When I first got that ill-fated data-analyst job, I drove a rusty Subaru that creaked like it was a few blocks from disintegrating into scrap metal. I also wrote a student-loan check every month that left me a pittance to live on. More than once, my take-home dinner was frosted donuts left over from a work meeting. Because raises substantially reduced my financial anxiety and filled my dinner plate with warm meals, they motivated me. But by the time I sat on Jo Ann's couch to resign, I had a reliable car and cans of chili in the cupboard. One more raise would have been an ineffective motivator.

Today, economists have appropriately downgraded the role of extrinsic rewards. Unfortunately, the vast majority of us regular people remain stuck in the practices, if not the beliefs, of our ill-informed past. The proverbial dangling carrot remains pervasive in our job negotiations, incentive structures and performance reviews. Eighty-five percent of U.S. large employers still expect employees to work harder when financially incentivized.[17] Similarly, even when we know that pay won't make a job more attractive than a lower-paying alternative, most of us still choose the higher-paying jobs we like less.[18]

We've been so duped into assuming that pay and perks motivate us that we don't realize its absurdity. Let's imagine we are doing a work task. It might be creating a spreadsheet or building a ramp. Would we think, "If I lived in a mansion instead of a studio apartment, this task would be more enjoyable"? Of course not. If there is any connection between the fanciness of the abode we can afford and the pleasure we get from ordering spreadsheet columns or hammering nails, it's a convoluted and weak one. Sure, a pay raise is a mechanism for owning a mansion, but having a mansion to go home to doesn't meaningfully affect the task at hand. Extrinsic rewards leave the work itself unimproved. Thus, our attitude toward work is also unimproved.

More Limitations of Money

It's established that owning a mansion doesn't improve our work experience, but it might still lift our spirits after work. Doesn't money increase life satisfaction? Kahneman partnered with his Princeton University colleague, Angus Deaton, to answer this question. After studying 450,000 people, they uncovered that income does increase our happiness and wellbeing—up to about $75,000 per year.[19] Beyond this amount, additional income does not increase happiness.

It might take $10,000 more than it took in 2010, when Kahneman and Deaton's research was published, to hit the limit of money-bought happiness. Furthermore, the exact figure varies by location and individual. But the precise dollar amount at which money stops improving our emotional wellness is irrelevant. The useful conclusion is that money's positive impact on happiness is similar to its effect on motivation. It fizzles out at the point where money provides us survival and safety.

It's hard to fathom how our expectations of money could have become so misguided. Yet, historically speaking, it's quite common that millions of educated people fall for a false belief because a group of experts got it wrong. Consider these five notions: identifying witches based on buoyancy, eating margarine because it's healthy, enslaving other human beings because we thought them inferior, considering California an island and assuming that Earth is at the center of the universe. If we were in another time, most of us would have believed these seriously wrongheaded notions. They were widely accepted ideas for decades—some for centuries. At every point in history, some portion of commonly held beliefs and actions are mistaken. As fond as I am of those of us alive now, we're no exception. We expect that obtaining money will do more for us than it ever could.

Our assumption that pay will improve work and life is not merely wrong. It's damaging. We think we are climbing toward higher fulfillment with each raise when, in reality, we're spinning in circles at the bottom rung of life's rewards. That's not to say there's anything wrong with securing a raise. There isn't. But we shouldn't expect additional wealth to make getting out of bed for work any easier. What undermines our job motivation and satisfaction is not that we pursue money, it's that we don't pursue loftier goals.

Chapter 3

AIMING HIGHER

As already established, it was actually wise of me to decline pay as a remedy for my demotivation and dissatisfaction. (Well, okay, it was wise of Dirk.) Yet, my quitting remains puzzling. I rejected not only a raise, but also the analytics work that I once enjoyed and expected to enjoy again. I also gave up an enriching community of coworkers. Finally, I walked away from opportunities to take on new challenges and develop my skills. One could say that I gave up passion, people and progress. Upon closer inspection, the younger me still sounds a tad irrational.

The Midrange Motivators: Passion, People and Progress

Studies find that passion, people and progress motivate us more effectively than pay and perks do.[20] When a performance bonus no longer lures us to the office, a project we love (passion), new friend (people) or challenging goal (progress) might. Why was this bounty of benefits still not enough for the under-30 me? What kind of a malcontent was I?

I was an ordinary human malcontent. Passion, people and progress only motivate until we meet these needs. They are a rung above pay and perks, but not the top rung. If you think I'm appropriating Abraham Maslow's theory of successively higher-order needs, you're right. The twentieth-century psychologist helped us understand that once we meet a need, we have to pursue a higher need to stay motivated. I've merely updated his theory per recent research findings. Work that delivers passion, people and progress still falls short of the mightiest reward and, in time, leaves us with a nagging sense of dissatisfaction. Jo Ann's offer of a more challenging project was not an effective lure because my need for progress was met. So were my needs for passion and people. More of these would not motivate me. I needed something else.

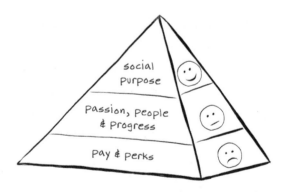

Hierarchy of Motivation

The Ultimate Motivator: Social Purpose

During one particular week in each of the last ten years, the New York Yankees won, on average, 74 percent of games. If you're not as embarrassingly infatuated with baseball as I am, you might not realize this is astonishing. It easily beats their 57 percent winning average during that decade. In fact, it beats every major league team's winning percentage back to 1954. The Yankees are at home during the week in question, but homefield advantage doesn't explain their success. The average winning percentage during that week is still 10 percentage points higher than the decade's homefield winning percentage (74 percent versus 64 percent).[21] What, then, explains this week's outrageous success? (No, fellow Red Sox fans, it's not that the Yankees are trouncing our team.)

The Yankees' exceptional record during this one week is likely due to what's at the top of the Hierarchy of Motivation. Psychologists call it "eudaimonic purpose." Because I almost pulled a muscle trying to pronounce that word, I use a synonym: "social," as in relating to societal good. Social—or eudaimonic—purpose is pursuing meaningful contributions to others or to a societal cause. Helping low-income families access the beach is an act of social purpose. Attaining a pay raise, upgrading our job to better match our passions or otherwise pursuing what's on the bottom two levels of the Hierarchy of Motivation are self-oriented acts, what scientists call "hedonic" purpose.

The winning week is Yankees Helping Others Persevere & Excel (HOPE) Week. During this one week per season, players take field trips with individuals and families facing hardship. One year, for example, relief pitcher Dellin Betances and several teammates spent a day at the Bronx Zoo with an eleven-year-old boy fighting leukemia and his seven-year-old sister who donated bone marrow to her brother. When Betances did his job from the mound at Yankees stadium that evening, he didn't give up a single hit. It's likely that social purpose helped him succeed.

As covered earlier, in certain rare circumstances pay can motivate. Furthermore, pursuing passion, people and progress motivate across a broader set of circumstances and more effectively than pay. But all these hedonic pursuits are to social-purpose pursuits what a jeep is to a jet. We don't progress as fast or as far when fueled by hedonic pursuits as opposed to social purpose. One study, for example, compared workers who were told their work helped charitable causes with workers in identical jobs who weren't told this. Those who knew they were pursuing social purpose conducted equally high-quality work as those who didn't but were 24 percent faster and had 43 percent less downtime.[22] Another experiment studied workers scanning online images for specific patterns. One randomly selected subgroup was told that they were labeling tumor cells to assist medical researchers. The others were not given any context about the work. As in the case of the first experiment, workers who knew they were supporting the health of others processed more images than those who had no reason to believe their work promoted social purpose. In this case, however, there was a difference in quality. Despite producing more, the social-purpose workers had higher quality work.[23] Other research uncovered that the social-purpose performance boost is so evident that supervisors notice it.[24] Simply put, social purpose is our most powerful motivator.

Social purpose not only increases motivation and performance, it also makes us happier with our jobs. My research documented 13 percent higher job satisfaction, on average, in employees whose work experience incorporated social purpose than in those whose work didn't.[25] Other studies reached similar conclusions. The Happiness Research Institute in Copenhagen found that lack of workplace purpose is the biggest culprit in job dissatisfaction among Danes.[26] Another European study found that incorporating social purpose into work boosted job satisfaction within a month.[27] In fact, so many studies link social purpose to job satisfaction that researchers who systematically reviewed all the evidence say the relationship is indisputable.[28]

Notice that the definition of social purpose, "pursuing meaningful contributions to others or to a societal cause," includes the imprecise word "meaningful." What makes a contribution meaningful? Our judgement does. An action is a meaningful contribution to others or to a societal cause if we consider it so. Some might say helping wealthy individuals manage their finances in a way that minimizes their anxiety or saving cattle from the slaughterhouse are acts of social purpose. Others might disagree.

Despite our differences, my experience has led me to conclude that we disagree on only a paper-thin sliver of the possible acts of social purpose. Virtually all of us consider teaching children to read, removing trash from a beach, finding a cure for Alzheimer's disease and sheltering hurricane victims acts of social purpose, for example. Nevertheless, it's important to realize that social purpose is in the eyes of the beholder or, rather, in the heart of the beholder. We define our own social purpose.

Of course, there is the possibility that what we consider social purpose might not be helpful to others or to a societal cause. Even worse, it might do more damage than good. Fortunately, we can mitigate this risk. My experience tutoring Alex, a first-grade student with straight black hair down to his jaw, illustrates how.

Ensuring Our Social-Purpose Efforts Truly Contribute

It's February and I've been helping Alex learn to read since September. It's enjoyable to witness him get happier with every rereading of the same three books. But he's lagging in reading level and in danger of failing first grade. I, therefore, put his favorite books away and force him to read more advanced ones. In March, the teacher tells me that Alex doesn't want any more reading sessions and that he even cried about it. I'm shocked. He typically greets me by running full speed at me, hugging my waist and grinning. The grin remains throughout our forty-five minutes of reading. I thought our sessions were the highlight of his day. But I now realize he hasn't given me his full-contact hug in several weeks and has been somber during our sessions. I hadn't noticed that my social-purpose effort was making the person I'm trying to help miserable.

The teacher suggests that I stop focusing on helping Alex get a passing grade and instead help ensure that he develops a lifelong love of reading. Alex and I go back to rereading books he should have left behind months earlier, per the guideposts of the educational system. More importantly, I pay close attention to his emotional state and adjust my service accordingly. He again runs to greet me, grins any time he's holding an open book in his pudgy hands and reads with delight. But he fails first grade.

As my experience with Alex illustrates, sometimes it's hard to ensure that our efforts are truly helpful. I don't have a solution for what I consider one of humanity's most vexing tragedies: We can do something with the best intentions and, nevertheless, not be helpful (or worse). But I do believe we have a mechanism for discovering we aren't helping and, if needed, righting our way. It's the advice my father gave me: Listen for the whisper of the world's needs. I stopped helping Alex when I stopped listening to him.

In my two decades of witnessing and studying people's social-purpose efforts, I've noticed that the individuals most revered for their meaningful contributions are always listening and adjusting their social-purpose acts accordingly. They might start with ill-conceived efforts but quickly remedy them. In other words, if we listen to the needs of others as honestly and intently as we possibly can, over time, most of our acts of social purpose will become genuine contributions. Alex's second time through first grade went well. He happily read more difficult books with me, got high marks across all subjects and started second grade with a fondness for reading.

You Are Too Wonderful for Lame Work

Dirk's statement that I was too wonderful for lame work was more insightful than either of us knew. My analyst job was "lame" per Merriam-Webster's second definition of "lacking needful or desirable substance."[29] Specifically, it lacked the social purpose I unknowingly needed. Instead of bringing out the best in me, my job nudged me toward the unmotivated, underproductive and uninspired worker that I had devolved to. It left me stalled halfway up the Hierarchy of Motivation because it was devoid of the most potent and enduring driver of work motivation, performance and satisfaction: social purpose. Although Dirk and I are no longer married, his statement is still relevant. In fact, it's a universal truth. We're *all* too wonderfully purpose-oriented to be at jobs that don't contribute to the world. Make no mistake. Dirk's statement applies to you: "You are too wonderful for lame work."

You are too wonderful
for lame work.

-Dirk

The Impact Social Purpose Has on Our Personal Lives

I'm on stage in Atlanta facing 350 awards-banquet attendees. I start my keynote by asking participants to assess how stressed they feel on a scale of one to ten, with one being "not at all" and ten being "extremely." Then I ask them to do a work-related charitable act that takes no more than five minutes and costs no more than five dollars. At first, I get quizzical looks. But soon the ballroom buzzes with people posting a LinkedIn testimonial for a laid-off colleague, donating to a coworker's fundraising run or calling their receptionist to thank him for being dependable.

At the conclusion of the five minutes, I ask participants to, again, note their stress level using the same scale. I then ask those whose stress increased to please stand. One woman, which rounds to zero percent of the audience, pops up. Next, I ask those whose stress remained the same to stand. Approximately 20 percent of attendees do. Finally, I ask those whose stress dropped to stand. The entire rest of the room, approximately 80 percent of participants, jump up. As if to drive the point home, most are smiling and a few holler "woo hoo!"

I've discussed how social purpose improves job motivation, performance and satisfaction which, in turn, improves our overall life happiness. However, this is just half the social-purpose story. There is evidence that social purpose is like an elixir for our personal lives as well. Specifically, social purpose appears to help us in the eight ways that follow.

1. **Social Purpose Reduces Stress**

Atlanta residents are among the most hospitable in the world, but that's not why they responded positively to my quirky test. I've conducted the above exercise in Las Vegas, London, Los Angeles, Madrid, Mexico City, New York, Saint Paul, Toronto and on webinars with global audiences. In every case, the vast majority of participants reported a reduction in stress after their simple act of social purpose.

As humans, they can't help it. The social-purpose stress drop is a physiological response outside of their control. Imaging of the brain reveals that acts of social purpose reduce the stress response at the cellular level.[30] This explains why researchers have documented that pursuing social purpose lowers the amount of stress we experience from final exams, financial woes or other concerns.[31] By posting recommendations, saying kind words or otherwise making small contributions to others, my audience members unknowingly relaxed their brains.

My experience is that no matter how much evidence we have, many of us can't fathom how a simple act of charity can have such a powerful and instant effect—until we experience it. Therefore, I encourage you to spend the next five minutes replicating the exercise my Atlanta audience did: Assess your level of stress on the ten-point scale, do a small act of social purpose and assess your level of stress again. It's extremely likely that your stress will drop. Even if it doesn't (typically because you weren't stressed to begin with), your small charitable act might have heightened your wellness in the seven other ways that follow.

2. **Social Purpose Improves Mental Health**

Since feeling stress is often related to the more serious affliction of experiencing anxiety, one would expect that social purpose helps protect us against anxiety. A study on youth found that it does.[32] But this is only the beginning of the positive mental-health effects social purpose appears to have. Research suggests that acts of social purpose are one factor (among many, including genetics, exercise and diet) that reduce our chances of addiction, depression, life dissatisfaction, emotional exhaustion and low self-worth.[33]

Acts of social purpose might even lower the probability of having and acting on suicidal thoughts. Again, many factors reduce our risk of suicide, but a study of nearly 140,000 people across 130 countries found that social purpose appears to be one of them. Social purpose helps to explain why some countries with widespread poverty but where people routinely help others, like Senegal, have lower suicide rates than richer countries where acts of social purpose are less common, like France.[34] Austrian Holocaust survivor, psychologist and author of the classic book, *Man's Search for Meaning*, Victor Frankl, put it this way, "There is nothing in the world, I venture to say, that would so effectively help one to survive even the worst conditions as the knowledge that there is a meaning in one's life."[35]

Nothing...would so effectively help one to survive even the worst conditions as the knowledge that there is a meaning in one's life.

-Viktor Frankl

3. Social Purpose Improves Physical Health

Researchers randomly divided seventy-three older individuals suffering from high blood pressure into two groups. One group was given $120 and instructed to spend $40 on themselves every week for three weeks. Members of the other group were also given $120 but asked to spend $40 on others every week. At the completion of the experiment, the self-oriented spenders had no change in blood pressure. The social-purpose spenders experienced a blood pressure drop as large as medication or exercise would have generated.[36] In another study, researchers randomly divided a group of adolescents into two groups, one volunteered for charitable causes and the other did not. Four months later, those who volunteered had lower cholesterol than those who hadn't.[37]

The above studies are on cardiovascular health, but social purpose appears to improve other aspects of health as well. There are studies linking acts of social purpose to reductions in inflammation, infectious disease and obesity, for example.[38]

4. Social Purpose Reduces Pain

In cases when acts of social purpose don't spare us from physical ailments, they might still reduce the associated pain. Academics have scanned the brains of individuals whose hands received a mild electric shock. Individuals who had just done an act of social purpose showed a lower pain response in the brain than those who hadn't.[39] In another study, the same researchers asked cancer patients living with chronic pain to cook and clean for either themselves or for others at their treatment center. When they were helping others, their pain levels were lower than when they were helping themselves.[40]

5. Social Purpose Appears to Boost Popularity

Dozens of studies find that those of us who pursue social purpose have higher quality friendships, more social connections, better reputations, more popularity and happier romantic relationships than those of us who don't pursue social purpose.[41]

6. Social Purpose Increases Happiness

Research conducted on brain activity suggests that serotonin, dopamine and oxytocin are what made my Atlanta audience smile and yelp after their charitable acts.[42] In other words, social purpose rewards us with the same feel-good chemicals that sex and dessert do. Studies conducted outside the laboratory confirm the existence of this "helper's high" in women, men, elderly individuals, members of traditional societies, criminals and seemingly every demographic group imaginable across over 130 countries.[43] Acts of social purpose appear to increase happiness even if we find ourselves in that wretched stretch of life known as adolescence.[44]

One study found that those who perform workplace acts of social purpose go to bed happier than those who don't.[45] Another study compared people asked to do three nice things per week for themselves to people asked to do three nice things per week for others or a cause. For example, a participant in the first (hedonic) group treated themselves to a meal at their favorite restaurant. In contrast, a participant in the second (social-purpose) group helped an elderly individual with her grocery shopping. After four weeks, those in the social-purpose group benefitted from an increase in happiness, but those in the hedonic group did not.[46] Other studies reached similar conclusions.[47] Furthermore, the impact that doing a few social-purpose acts has on happiness is considerable. It is so sizable that observers easily detect it and it can last two or more weeks.[48]

7. **Social Purpose Appears to Extend Lifespan**

Studies find that a couple of hours of social-purpose activity a week reduces our chances of dying in any given year by 24 percent.[49] Of course, this isn't surprising. If social purpose is associated with reductions in stress, anxiety, heart disease, inflammation and infectious diseases, how could it *not* be associated with reduced mortality?

8. **Social Purpose Appears to Boost Career Success**

A study of more than 2,000 professionals discovered that doing work with a social purpose is associated with a 10 percent increase in the possibility of receiving a raise.[50] Similarly, research finds that those who routinely perform small acts of social purpose are 40 percent more likely to get a promotion.[51] This makes sense. Surely, being more motivated, productive and satisfied at work—as well as healthier, better liked and happier in life—confers an advantage in making more money and achieving greater success.

There is a caveat to the above findings. Not all of them *prove* that acts of social purpose cause these personal benefits. Because of methodological limitations, some of the cited research only shows that studied individuals who perform acts of social purpose have better health and wellness versus those who do not and that the *most likely* explanation is their social-purpose activity. In some cases, more research is needed to confirm causality. Nevertheless, we should not overstate the limitations of the full complement of studies. The body of existing research unequivocally establishes that social purpose substantially improves our health and wellness, including lowering our risk of suffering from stress, depression, cardiovascular disease and unhappiness. The impact of social purpose varies by demographics but applies to the human species as a whole (with the possible exception of sociopaths). Cardiologist Alan Rozanski from the Icahn School of Medicine at Mount Sinai in New York City summarizes the evidence with, "The need for meaning and purpose is…the deepest driver of wellbeing there is."[52]

The need for meaning and purpose is... the deepest driver of wellbeing there is.

-Alan Rozanski

Caring for others does not conflict with caring for ourselves, as many of us believe. On the contrary, the plethora of evidence presented above suggests that *not* caring for others is a form of self-neglect. In fact, researchers at Stockholm University and Anglia Ruskin University found intriguing evidence that the more physiologically in touch we are with ourselves, the more social purpose we naturally pursue. Specifically, a 10 percent higher ability to detect our heartbeats, what scientists call "interoceptive sensitivity," corresponds to 16 percent higher donations to societal causes.[53] It's as if our hearts are telling us that social purpose is good for us, but most of us can't hear our deepest selves through the bustle of our outer lives.

Social Purpose Is the New Exercise

What if social purpose helped us get fit and lean? Sorry, but there is no evidence that it does. We still need to hop on our bikes or lace our running shoes and get moving. The history of exercise, however, provides a helpful metaphor.

One hundred years ago, exercise was considered an unnecessary complication to life. If anything, it was thought to be injurious, especially to women. Half a century ago, scientists had amassed enough evidence to establish that movement was central to a healthy life. At that time, ordinary people were becoming aware of the importance of exercise but were mostly sitting on their rear ends, *not* exercising.

Social purpose is where exercise was five decades ago. Psychologists, evolutionary biologists, behavioral economists, public-health researchers and other relevant specialists know that social purpose is central to human wellness. We ordinary people are increasingly aware of our need for social purpose and suspect that our workplaces are the place to meet it. For example, research I helped conduct found that 48 percent of Fortune 1000 employees consider work that has social purpose very important, a higher percentage than those who say the same about training opportunities (40 percent) and paid family leave (39 percent).[54] Unfortunately, employers aren't meeting our need for social purpose. Although they are migrating in that direction, their moves are too broad-brush to brighten the halls we sweep or the cubicles we sit in.

Companies across the globe are redefining themselves in terms of meaningful contributions to societal causes. For example, General Motors updated its vision statement in 2017 from, "To be the world leader in transportation products and related services" to "Zero crashes. Zero emissions. Zero congestion." Similarly, the Starbucks mission statement is, "To inspire and nurture the human spirit—one person, one cup and one neighborhood at a time." Some have said that capitalism is in a "purpose revolution."[55] But the corporate shift toward designing a perfectly safe car, helping customers thrive or other social purpose rarely affects our cleaning, computer work or whatever labor we do. Gallup finds that the majority of U.S. workers don't know what purpose their employer stands for. A study of one organization found the majority of employees believed its corporate mission and vision statements were solely meant for managers.[56] The corporate response to the need for work with social purpose has left most of our daily labor as devoid of social purpose as ever.

Those of us who aren't in leadership positions, especially, are left in a frustrating limbo. We are awakened to our yearning for workplace social purpose but are unsure how to act on it. We could switch careers and become a counselor, teacher or other do-good professional. Many of us, however, chose our jobs because we are attracted to the field or craft. We don't want to forgo fashion design to stand in front of third graders or leave behind tinkering with jet engines to counsel quarreling couples. We, thus, mostly stay at our jobs despite our unmet need for social purpose. Research studies on U.S. and global workers find the majority of us have work that does not meet our need for social purpose.[57] Fortunately, there are ways each one of us can ignite social purpose in our workweek, including those of us with limited authority, as presented in the upcoming section two.

Please don't get the impression that our only need is social purpose. While it's true that its absence undermines our wellness, social purpose cannot replace other human needs, including exercise, social connections, sleep, food, shelter, water and air. Instead, think of social purpose as the "new exercise"—a recently discovered human need to add to the shortlist.

The Promise of Social Purpose

As I walk down the hallway to my father's office, managers, engineers and clerks offer beaming compliments. I feel as admired as Amelia Earhart must have felt after her cross-Atlantic flight. Yet, I haven't done anything noteworthy, am eight years old and the praise is about my father. Still, it's impossible not to relish the warm shower of admiration.

Some of the praise is about Papi's professional competencies. "Dr. Boccalandro is a brilliant engineer." "Tony is my best hire." "Your dad's a fair and fun boss." "Your dad will be president someday."

Just as much praise, however, is about his social purpose. "When my wife's pregnancy had complications, your father personally boxed and delivered my office so I could be by her bedside and not lose my job." "Your dad stayed until midnight last week to help me with an urgent assignment, and I'm not even on his team!" "Tony is the only manager who drove into the slums to take workers home when there was a public-transportation strike."

Papi was known for two characteristics that many of us believe negate each other: success and compassion. Science, however, suggests that this isn't a contradiction. On the contrary, Papi's focus on contributing to others drove his career success. What's more, Papi was a happy worker and a fulfilled person. He was so animated about his job that we kids sat around the dinner table as he ate late at night, begging him for "work stories." In between bites of T-bone steak and gulps of gin and tonic, he would tell us about bosses, meetings and progress at construction sites.

On Christmas Day later that year, I find my father at the dining-room table writing furiously with a black felt-tip pen on a yellow legal pad. Seeing me hover next to him, he tells me that the proposed addition of guardrails on a major Venezuelan freeway will eliminate the livelihood of the families that cook and sell food off the side of the road. "We need to save these family-run roadside businesses. Any thoughts?" he asks. I don't have any, so I try to lure him into opening his presents. He says, "Thank you, *mi cielito lindo* [my precious little sky], I'll get to them" and goes back to writing. I'm surprised that what I consider the highlight of the year, playing with the toys Santa brought, can't pull Papi away from his work.

Decades later, I'm no longer surprised. I've now seen the evidence showing that if we have the courage to listen for the world's needs and to respond through our work, as Papi did, we can revel in a job so captivating it feels like play.

II. JOB PURPOSING: DO GOOD AT WORK TO DO GREAT IN LIFE

Chapter 4

WHAT JOB PURPOSING IS

"*I* love my work because I get to slay dragons!" says Dawn.

Dawn is not a hero in a fantasy novel. She's a Florida FedEx driver not much taller than a parking meter. By "dragons," Dawn means Burmese pythons. Many pet pythons, a species not native to Florida, have slithered into the wilderness, bred with each other and spawned an environmental calamity. Tens of thousands of wild pythons eat unsuspecting native creatures and threaten entire species of birds. In response, organizations like the Nature Conservancy and the Florida Fish and Wildlife Conservation Commission train people to travel wilderness roads, identify pythons, contact the local authorities and help remove these invasive snakes. This is where Dawn comes in. She serves as a trained python patroller as she crisscrosses the state delivering FedEx packages.

Like my father adding a pedestrian bridge for low-income families to a road blueprint, Dawn adjusted her job in a way that allows her to do good at work. Below are others who have done the same.

- A parking attendant named Leroy inspects tires and, if the tread is bald, alerts the car's owner. Leroy combats highway fatalities with every car he parks.

- A manufacturing-plant manager, Mike, donates ten dollars from his department's budget to a local food pantry every day his team has no safety violations. Mike's team members fight hunger every time they strap on a hardhat or hold a ladder for a colleague.

- A work-at-home employee at a professional-services business who competes in triathlons emails weekly tips to interested colleagues on how to adopt healthy behaviors. She's helping people be healthier on a weekly basis.

- The administrative assistant to the marketing director at a regional bank orders catering only from restaurants that support organic local farmers. Her meeting planning supports sustainable family farming.

- Having learned the storage facility where she works is closing for the foreseeable future due to the COVID-19 pandemic, the attendant spends her last workday calling every elderly customer to offer free delivery of anything they need to ride out the crisis. She delivered disaster relief on her commute home.

Even celebrities slant their labor toward social purpose. Oprah Winfrey discussed meaningful societal issues on her television program, like addiction and domestic violence, when other talk-show hosts broadcast sensationalism. Later, she added a book club to promote adult literacy.

By doing good from work, my father, Dawn, Leroy, Mike, Oprah and the other workers listed above have done what I've termed "job purposing."[58] Job purposing is any meaningful contribution to others or to a societal cause done as part of our work experience. Put another way, job purposing is a work-related action that, from the point of view of the individual performing it, furthers social purpose. More simply, job purposing is the application of the advice I give in speeches: If your job doesn't improve the world, improve your job.

If your job doesn't improve the world, improve your job.

-Bea Boccalandro

The research presented in chapters one through three suggests that job purposing has likely raised the work motivation, satisfaction and performance—as well as the personal wellbeing—of the above workers. They certainly see it this way. While Dawn had always liked her job, she credits job purposing with her newfound eagerness to get to work. Leroy, the parking attendant, was thrilled his colleagues expanded the tire inspection to a formal five-point safety check (including taillights, headlights, etc.) and believes being the originator of this program helped him get promoted to garage manager. The work-at-home service employee said that helping coworkers get healthier refreshed her work just when it was beginning to get unbearably dull. The administrative assistant who supports sustainable agriculture told me, "It's hard to feel significant around executives who make decisions involving millions of dollars. Leaving my own positive imprint makes me feel like I'm also important." Yet, Oprah's story of social purpose driving runaway success might be the most telling.

Oprah was born to unwed teenage parents in rural Mississippi, grew up in poverty, suffered from child abuse and is obviously a woman and a minority. Despite such underprivileged beginnings, she has built one of the most successful television careers of all time and amassed a $2.5 billion personal fortune.[59] Does she credit some of this success to her focus on social purpose? So much so that she advises, "The key to realizing a dream is to focus not on success but on significance."[60]

The key to realizing a dream is to focus not on success but on significance.

-Oprah Winfrey

To be clear, job purposing cannot fix every workplace issue. It won't remedy dangerous or hostile working conditions, poor management, exploitation, harassment or corruption. Job purposing remedies one specific and relatively high-order deficiency: work that doesn't meaningfully contribute to the world. While it's true that remedying this deficiency cascades into colossal positive impacts on our success and wellbeing, it still doesn't address any separate and distinct workplace problems like those listed above. Furthermore, some of these other issues are graver and more urgent than job purposing and should, thus, be prioritized.

When Studs Terkel, from chapter one, discovered that many saw work as a "sort of dying," he also discovered that the opposite is possible. His full quote is, "Work is about a search for daily meaning as well as daily bread, for recognition as well as cash, for astonishment rather than torpor; in short, for a sort of life rather than a Monday through Friday sort of dying."[61] Job purposing is the way to unlock the rewarding, meaningful and astonishing life that work can offer.

Work is about a
search for daily
meaning as well
as daily bread...
for a sort of life
rather than a
Monday through
Friday sort of dying.

-Studs Terkel

How to Know If We've Successfully Job Purposed

Most of us intuitively know if our jobs are purposed. In fact, that's the definition of job purposing: feeling confident that, as part of our workweek, we've made a meaningful contribution to others or to a cause.

It doesn't take altruistic heroics to have a positive impact and to *feel* like we have. For example, Verena Rentrop knew beyond a doubt that she made a meaningful contribution at her technology job at Nokia. Yet, her job purposing couldn't have been simpler. She filled a box with tasty treats and spent lunchtime walking from desk to desk offering a smile, a snack and a few seconds of undivided attention, what she calls "micro-moments of love." My first conversation with Verena convinced me that she *must* have a purposed job. She's the poster child for the benefits of pursuing social purpose. She's energetic, cheerful, seemingly healthy and as delightful as the flower pattern on her dress. I wanted my talk with her never to end.

Verena's example of sharing treats is a modest action that contributes to others or a societal cause. Other workers have job purposed by updating email signatures to bring attention to a neglected charitable cause, inviting colleagues to eliminate single-use plastics from their workday, showing interest in every person they speak with and otherwise doing small other-oriented acts.

After I present the above explanation of job purposing, people often ask me something like, "That's it? How can such minor adjustments, often at the outer edges of our jobs, change how motivated, productive and satisfied we are with work? Are you delusional?" Okay, they don't verbalize that last question, but their scrunched eyebrows give it away. I don't blame them. At first, I didn't believe the evidence either and some of it came from my own research.

A Little Purpose Goes a Long Way

I have job-purposing data from hundreds of thousands of workers across dozens of companies and countries. For 74 percent of respondents, five to thirty minutes of workplace social-purpose activity during the prior week is enough for them to report that their job is purposed. That is, they feel they make meaningful contributions to others or a societal cause as part of their workplace experience. As would be expected, the workers with purposed jobs are more motivated and satisfied with work than those without.

Others have corroborated my findings. One experiment asked workers to direct mini acts of job purposing toward coworkers for one month. These acts were as simple and small as buying a coworker a coffee or listening to their stories with more care. The study found that five of these small acts per month were enough to trigger higher levels of job satisfaction (compared to a control group).[62] Similarly, other research finds that episodic and short-lived social purpose moments, such as redirecting plastic waste from a landfill to recycling or helping a colleague understand a work-related concept, are enough for workers to describe their work as making a meaningful contribution.[63] Remember that my Atlanta audience reported feeling less stressed after a five-minute act of social purpose.

In other words, although a minority of us have purposed jobs, it typically takes only a few minutes per week of social-purpose activity to give ourselves this gift and reap its associated professional and personal benefits. Even monthly or quarterly job purposing boosts our success and wellbeing, although less substantially than a weekly cadence does.

Of course, job purposing can be as ambitious as we choose to make it. For example, a handful of factory workers at a Unilever beauty-products factory in India started a cosmetology course in their village to help local women get a job while also selling Unilever products. Hundreds of women have graduated from their training center and most have secured jobs in the beauty industry.

A second example of ambitious job purposing comes from Alberto Vollmer, co-owner of the Santa Teresa rum distillery in Venezuela. Vollmer offered the gang that robbed his business and almost killed an employee an alternative to jail time. They could work at Santa Teresa and repay the damage they caused. The gang members chose employment. This started Santa Teresa on a job-purposing journey that, seventeen years later, has resulted in a comprehensive rehabilitation and jobs program. Santa Teresa now offers at-risk and incarcerated youth counseling, formal education, rugby, job apprenticeships and seemingly anything else they need to secure gainful employment at Santa Teresa or elsewhere. In other words, one of the world's top-ten rum producers doubles as a workforce development center that has helped tens of thousands of underprivileged youth become legally employed.

In summary, job purposing is highly elastic. It can be a high-stakes effort applied across our company's operations, as the Unilever team and Vollmer demonstrate. But it can also be a quick and comfortable action performed by one or two of us, as python-patrol Dawn and safety-check Leroy show. Both the grand and modest versions of job purposing—and everything in between—meaningfully contribute to others and ourselves. In other words, job purposing on any scale is worthwhile.

Chapter 5

WHAT JOB PURPOSING IS NOT

I'm sprawled on the living-room carpet as though I just landed an indoor belly flop. A magazine and drawing pad lay in front of me. I see Papi's loafers just before he sits down. Once awkwardly seated next to me, he examines my crayon drawing and breaks into song. *"Tengo una vaca lechera, no es una vaca cualquiera…"* (Which translates to "I have a dairy cow, it's not just any cow…")

"Papi, help! My second cow looks like it's kneeling." I whine. He's the right person to ask. Besides being able to do anything, in my eight-year-old judgment, I've seen him tilt his head to examine a photograph, put his felt-tip marker on paper and with a handful of strokes draw whatever was in the photograph—a woman getting out of a car, a man laughing, a monkey eating a mango. His drawing is always simpler, funnier and better than the photograph. I'm trying to do a "Papi drawing" of a photograph of cattle in a field.

"And what's wrong with a kneeling cow? How else is it supposed to pray?" Papi responds.

"Paaaapi, I'm not kidding. Look how terrible it looks," I counter.

"Hmmm. I see the problem. Your cow is naked! And praying? That's blasphemous. Quick! Draw a skirt!" he says with mock seriousness.

I giggle.

Papi clears his throat. "*Mi cielito lindo* [my precious little sky], to delineate something it helps to look at what's just outside of it," he says. He points to the space behind the animal's hard-to-draw front legs and under its belly. He then guides my hand to that place on the drawing and says, "Don't focus on the cow. Pay attention to the neighboring shapes." It does the trick. By drawing the contours of the area that abuts the cow with a bold line, I suddenly have a clearly defined and upright cow.

My dad's tip is helpful in understanding job purposing. Job purposing becomes clear when we define two concepts that are next door to and often confused with it: our life's purpose and our personal passion. Many people lament they can't job purpose because they don't know what their life's purpose is or what they are passionate about. Fortunately, these deficiencies are not a detriment to job purposing. They aren't even deficiencies, as I'll cover next.

You Don't Need a Life Purpose

Dawn, the FedEx driver, has been advised to find her life's purpose. Yet, she openly admits that she doesn't have one. Even after helping to rid the environment of an invasive species for over a year, she does not consider this cause her life's purpose. That's normal. Evolution shaped her and all of us into creatures meant to help many causes.

Imagine a pair of hunters, Stu and Hal, around 20,000 years ago. Crossing a river, Hal struggles in the current. Stu's life purpose is hunger relief. So, he says, "Sorry, buddy, water safety is not my life's purpose," and walks away from his drowning colleague. Such a single-minded focus would lead to Hal's death. Generalized to the entire population of prehistoric humans, it would lead to many deaths and extinction. Evolutionary forces have, therefore, *not* hardwired us to focus on one social purpose. Instead, we are designed to care about, and contribute toward, the full panoply of human vulnerabilities. Stu is moved to help Hal, whether he's drowning, hobbling from an injury or prostrate from illness.

After helping thousands of workers ignite a sense of purpose at work, I'm convinced that the quest to uncover one's "life purpose," or any singular way to contribute to the world, is unnatural and unhelpful. It's true that some people in some circumstances do well with one primary social purpose for part or all of their lives, such as reversing the climate crisis or ridding the planet of domestic violence. Almost always, however, these individuals were moved to pursue that issue precisely because they were open to detecting new needs around them. Furthermore, they remain open to opportunities to contribute in other ways and frequently do. After Hal's near-drowning, Stu might teach all tribe members to swim and become known as the water-safety guy. Even so, when his daughter spends a night writing from an upset stomach, he might say that food safety is also of interest.

In other words, insisting on a singular life purpose makes as much sense as eating one food. It limits our lives. If Dawn had decided that curing breast cancer or spreading her faith was her single life's purpose, she might have declined the opportunity to become a python patroller and would not love going to work every morning. If my father had narrowly committed himself only to giving impoverished individuals beach access, he would not have seen the opportunity to help coworkers or roadside entrepreneurs.

Those of us who happen to have a life purpose don't need to abandon it. Provided it doesn't limit our ability to detect and act on opportunities to contribute, it won't undermine job purposing. Those of us who don't have a life purpose, however, are not deficient. On the contrary, we are well-positioned to job purpose and enjoy a rewarding life that contributes in numerous and evolving ways.

Job Purposing Is Not the Same as Following Our Passion

Chopping chives, frying fish, beating batter or otherwise fixing food makes me despondent. I dislike having sticky hands, feeling splattering oil, inhaling puffs of flour and seemingly every other culinary sensation. If my job were cooking, I would be miserable. What if, however, my kitchen work was job purposed? What if I cooked at a café that stayed open an additional hour to offer free meals to families who would otherwise not eat that evening?

I would still want to pull my hair out.

Yes, I, the purpose advisor, admit that social purpose won't fix my cooking-induced misery. That's not to say that the purposed version of my odious job wouldn't be more motivating and engaging than the purpose-deprived version. Per the findings presented earlier, it would. Still, job purposing won't make me passionate about cooking.

Purpose and passion are distinct positive attributes of a job. Morten Hansen, a management professor at the University of California, Berkeley, explains the difference as, "Passion is 'do what you love,' while purpose is 'do what contributes.'"[64]

The ideal is to have both passion and purpose. Hansen's five-year research on 5,000 workers uncovered that people with both passion and purpose place in the 80th percentile in performance, on average, per supervisor ratings. If we take passion away but still have purpose, average performance drops to the 64th percentile. Based on her description of "liking, but not loving driving," Dawn, the FedEx python patroller, appears to fall into this group. While it leaves room for improvement, the 64th percentile is not low performance.

If we take purpose away but still have passion, on the other hand, we do end up underperforming: in the 20th percentile of performance, to be precise.[65] This is where we find workers who do what they find enjoyable—be it skiing, designing logos or forecasting sales—but their workdays lack social purpose. In other words, consistent with the Hierarchy of Motivation model from chapter three, purpose is a stronger driver of motivation and performance than passion.

So, I shouldn't get a kitchen job. But if I ever had to, I would absolutely need to job purpose. Otherwise, I would be setting myself up to perform near rock bottom.

Managing Work's Purpose and Passion

One morning, I find myself in a security-screening line at the Dallas airport. I witness the officer who checks identification, which includes date of birth, serenade a middle-aged woman with a quick and operatic rendition of the "Happy Birthday" song. I ask the singing officer, whose name is Aadesh, about his unusual customer service. He tells me that he loves music and is the lead singer and rhythm guitar player in a punk band. He explains that one evening two years earlier, he sang Happy Birthday to a young man who moved with difficulty and appeared to have "one of those muscular diseases." The young man told Aadesh that he was the only person who had acknowledged his birthday and thanked him through watery eyes.

Since hearing that heartbreaking comment from the disabled man, Aadesh has never skipped the opportunity to serenade customers on their birthday, even if he only has time for a few bars. Every day, several people thank him through teary eyes and, every few weeks, someone says that it's their only birthday greeting. A few passengers have even brought him home-baked cookies and other gifts on subsequent trips. The female officer next to Aadesh jumps into the conversation, "It's shocking how many people yearn for a little kindness on their birthday…but even if they don't, Aadesh's mini-serenades only improve their special day."

Aadesh leans toward me, grins and whispers, "Plus, I get to sing several times a day, and that's so much fun!" In other words, Aadesh found an elegant way to bring his passion into his work via job purposing. Using job purposing to align our jobs with our personal passions is a clever option available to some. If we can't find a way to make both passion and social purpose part of our work, though, the latter is still transformative (as covered in chapter three).

With or without a life purpose and with or without passion for our work, we can job purpose and reap the substantial benefits it bestows.

Chapter 6

A DOZEN WAYS TO JOB PURPOSE

I didn't need to quit my data-analyst job to start loving work again. I didn't need to give up my great supervisor, fun coworkers and interesting assignments. Had I known job purposing was an option, even the young and largely clueless me could have found a way.

I might have organized a workplace lunch-and-learn program on how anybody can help stem injustices toward migrant farmworkers, an issue closely related to the agricultural research I conducted. As part of the data analysis and reporting I did for organizations, I might have researched and recommended charitable causes for them to support. I might have enlisted colleagues in my workplace who owned cars to give rides to administrative staff members who endured two-hour bus commutes. I might have hired military veterans trying to enter the civilian workforce. Looking back, I see endless possibilities within that job for reigniting excitement for it. But, alas, I did not know what I was looking for. The few whispers of the world's needs that I *did* hear, such as the plight of migrant farmworkers and the grueling public-transportation commute of some staff members, didn't activate anything in me beyond a helpless ennui.

After taking a few jobs strangely similar to the one I left, I started to suspect that my father's rebellious workplace acts had pointed the way to fulfilling work, no matter the actual job. Therefore, I delved into the practicality of anybody in any job doing good at work and launched a consulting firm dedicated to this idea. Twenty years of implementing, measuring and learning from efforts to do good at work led me to the practice of job purposing. The workers at Aetna, Bank of America, Disney, DPR Construction, FedEx, HP, IBM, QVC, Western Digital and other companies have handed me thousands of examples of successful job purposing. I've distilled this bounty of ideas into the twelve most universally feasible job-purposing methods. Within each method, there are applications appropriate for large manufacturing plants, home offices and everything in between, even if we have limited authority.

Job Purposing Method 1: Tilt a Task Toward Social Purpose

When Papi added a beach bridge for low-income families in his highway blueprint, Dawn gave nature an assist as she delivered packages, Leroy warned drivers of dangerous tires and Oprah promoted adult literacy from her show, they purposed the very crux of their jobs. They upgraded core job tasks—designing, driving, parking and entertaining, respectively—to encompass social purpose.

Mike, the manufacturing-plant manager who donated ten dollars from his department's budget to the local food pantry every day his team had no safety violations, and the administrative assistant who scheduled department lunches at restaurants that sourced local organic produce also brought social purpose into job tasks. However, the tasks they purposed—managing safety issues and organizing lunches—were episodic. This also works.

Whether tasks are central or ancillary to the job, they can often be tilted toward social purpose as the examples below illustrate.

- A designer of surfboard fins equips them with sensors that relay location-specific data on water conditions to scientists. His product design helps ocean conservation.
- Window washers at pediatric hospitals wear Batman and other superhero costumes to delight hospitalized children.
- An internal auditor helps mitigate the stress her work generates in the teams she audits. In the introductory meeting, she acknowledges that being audited can produce anxiety. She covers a few stress-reduction practices and gives each team member a sprig of lavender, which she believes has a calming effect. She also learned to deliver bad news with respect and compassion and takes great care to apply these softening techniques when reporting negative findings. She now feels confident she minimizes the pain her work can cause.
- An instructor at an accounting firm replaces a written case study in his new-hire class with consulting assistance to a local nonprofit. Students help nonprofit representatives with their accounting challenges and the nonprofit benefits from free financial counseling.
- A human resources manager at a healthcare company scraps the dull information booth customarily used at college recruitment fairs and, instead, sets up a blood donation station with the local American Red Cross chapter and staffs it with company employees. In so doing, the company demonstrates its commitment to supporting the healthcare system and

students contribute to the health of others as they learn about the company.

Because it does good through commonplace activities, the job-purposing method of tilting a task toward social purpose typically has a high impact on those of us doing the job purposing and on the societal causes we are supporting. I, therefore, recommend trying this method first. But it's sometimes difficult and impractical to modify job tasks. Fortunately, we don't need to be concerned if we haven't found a way to apply this first method. There are eleven others.

Job Purposing Method 2: Help Coworkers With Their Work

I'm nine years old and wandering around a room full of cubicles looking for something to do while my father finishes a phone call from his nearby office. Marcos, a stout handyman I have met several times, sees me, sets down the floor lamp he was carrying and asks me if I've heard how my father saved his job. I shake my head. Marcos signals me to sit on a leather chair, but I choose to step on the chair and sit cross-legged atop someone's desk. He nods in approval and starts his story.

Toward the end of a long day and with his lower back cramping, Marcos spilled a pail of dirty water. Water not only filled the hallway but cascaded down nearby steps. He says that the commotion brought the "big-big boss" out of his office. The boss started yelling at Marcos, "What's wrong with you? Why can't you do anything right? Go back to your shantytown…" I suspect the boss used expletives, but Marcos is too proper to repeat those.

Marcos explains that my father, a director who reported to the big-big boss, appeared during the tirade. Papi walked into the puddle to stand next to Marcos and face their scolding senior leader. Papi made a palm-forward "stop" gesture and said to his boss, "It's okay. We all spill things. I'll make sure it's cleaned up." The boss retreated into his office.

My father then asked one of the many onlookers to get a mop and pail from the closet. When a young man returned with it, Papi started mopping the water and wringing it into the bucket with his bare hands. Marcos pleaded with him not to, believing such work was beneath a director, but Papi ignored him.

Another way to job purpose is to assist coworkers with their work. Most of us already help those on our work teams. Such teamwork is a foundation of high-performing companies and a fine form of job purposing. As Marcos' story illustrates, we can also help those in jobs that have nothing to do with ours. The following are examples of workers who job purpose by aiding coworkers, both near and far on the organizational chart.

- On nights when she can't sleep, a plant worker heads to her assembly line before the night shift ends and offers to finish the shift of anybody who needs to leave early. She says that she's gotten hugs and gifts from grateful migraine sufferers, sleep-deprived parents and even individuals who are hung over. On the rare occasions when she has no takers, she simply goes to the cafeteria to drink coffee and read the newspaper until her shift starts.
- When possible, a New York restaurant manager takes a break from office work to help the food-delivery drivers unload boxes of produce.
- A senior executive at an amusement park routinely encourages ride attendants to go enjoy a few rides while he covers for them.
- An office worker hand delivers all the documents sitting on the shared printer to his coworkers every time he collects his own.
- A commercial airline pilot helps the crew clean the plane after he's completed his post-flight duties.

- A receptionist at a financial-services firm tells individuals in the waiting area one thing she likes about the coworker they will meet. She might say, "Stuart is solid as a rock, one of the most reliable people I know." Her only goal was to make guests more comfortable, but her coworkers report that she is helping them close sales.

- A junior team member who is a whiz at creating slide decks holds web-based tech-support office hours for any fellow employee "victimized" by PowerPoint from 8:30 a.m. to 9:30 a.m. every Tuesday.

Clearly, opportunities to job purpose by supporting our coworkers abound.

Job Purposing Method 3: Advocate for a Cause

I climb into Kevin's Lyft vehicle. It has holes in the seat and reeks of day-old tuna fish. I wonder how it's possible that he has a perfect five-star rating.

After a few minutes of chit chat, Kevin asks if I know anybody with Down Syndrome. When I tell him that I don't, he says, "That's a shame!" He shares that his nine-year-old daughter Ava, who has Down Syndrome, is "a blessing to the world." He's so animated when he talks about this genetic disorder that I find myself asking many questions. Kevin teaches me that although individuals with Down Syndrome are cognitively impaired, they can usually become dedicated and productive employees. I've never considered hiring an individual with Down Syndrome, but I will now.

I ask Kevin how often he talks to passengers about Down Syndrome. "As often as I can!" he says. He explains that he won't disturb anybody absorbed by their electronic device or trying to rest. But he says that if he's already talking to a passenger, "Why not have a meaningful conversation instead of one about the weather?"

The way Kevin sees it, every person who leaves his vehicle with an appreciation for individuals with Down Syndrome makes it more likely that his daughter and others who are intellectually disabled will be treated with dignity throughout their lives. "If I didn't try to educate passengers, this job would feel like a pointless grind," he says. Kevin is experiencing what the research presented in chapter three found: Jobs that contribute to others or societal causes are more motivating than jobs that don't.

Kevin demonstrates that those of us who talk or write at work likely have the opportunity to build awareness and support for a societal issue. He further shows that we can do this without being annoying. Examples of job purposing through advocacy include:

- A self-described "100 percent Canadian Irishman" at a meeting in Toronto starts his presentation by honoring the Native Americans who inhabited the land he stands on. He says a few words about the tribe and invites attendees to sign a petition urging the Canadian government to honor its promises to indigenous people.
- A restaurant eliminates all the letter "b"s from its menu to bring awareness to the alarming decline in the world's bee population.
- A cashier wears a button that says, "Ask me how to tell if someone is having a stroke." When I ask, he gives me a small card with the acronym FAST and explains it to me. (F is for face, reminding us to ask the person to smile; A is for arms, reminding us to ask them to raise both arms; S is for speech, reminding us to ask the person to repeat a simple statement; and T is for time, reminding us to seek emergency medical

assistance if the person has difficulty with any of the three requests.) When I thank him, he says, "Thank *you*! Someone who made the effort to learn FAST, like you just did, saved my wife's life."

- A rock band, "The 1975," features climate activist Greta Thunberg delivering a speech on one of its songs.

- The Flamingo Las Vegas Hotel and Casino has a fifteen-acre bird sanctuary on the property that educates guests about flamingos and other rare birds.

- Bill, a conventions director with a penchant for history, gives free historical tours of the hotel where he works, which is on the National Historic Registry. When I ask him why, he answers, "I want my grandchildren to have historic buildings to marvel at."

- Levi Strauss & Co. worked with Goodwill Industries International to create "A Care Tag for Our Planet." After the customary instructions such as "machine wash in cold water," the tags on Levi's clothing now say, "donate to Goodwill when no longer needed and care for our planet."

In other words, there appears to be an infinite variety of ways to educate and, thus, do good at work through advocacy.

A few hours after my ride with Kevin, I open the Lyft email asking for my rating. I instinctively tap on five stars. Then I remember the foul condition of his vehicle and consider sliding my finger to a lower rating. Yet, after witnessing Kevin's passion for helping those with Down Syndrome, my objection to his car seems petty. I'm not the only one whose critical attitude is softened by acts of social purpose. Researchers have found that most of us are less likely to get angry and share our woes of bad service when the company pursues social purpose.[66] This might very well answer the question I asked myself upon entering Kevin's car: How could he possibly have a perfect five-star rating?

I hit submit and, despite his grubby vehicle, job-purposing Kevin gets another perfect review.

Job Purposing Method 4: Be Kinder than Necessary

Rick Warren asks an audience of hundreds of intent listeners, "Want to make a difference at work?" I'm at this Christian leader's talk on using "business as a mission to the world," precisely for his answer to that question. If anyone has a pragmatic response, it's Warren. His book, *The Purpose Driven Life*, sold 50 million copies across thirty languages and sat on *The New York Times* bestseller list for almost two years. What's Warren's advice on how to make a difference at work?

"Be kind" he says.

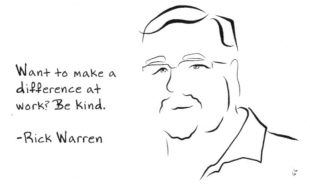

Want to make a
difference at
work? Be kind.

-Rick Warren

Arguably the world's top purpose evangelist suggests that we change the world by greeting coworkers by name, asking the delivery woman about her sick pet, listening to our client's stories and otherwise being a little sweeter.

If you think a small act of kindness can't possibly qualify as a meaningful contribution, you've been fortunate. You've never felt so broken that a barista's genuine interest in your prattling or coworker's playful wink is what prevents you from burrowing under your bed covers midafternoon convinced that the world is devoid of worth. I have felt that despondent. I know that, at least for some of us some of the time, a kind gesture can feel like a lifesaver. Even those of us who are not in such a fragile place will benefit from kindness. Making many people a smidgen happier is also a meaningful societal contribution. Below are examples of job purposing via kindness.

- As part of his route, a mail carrier rings the doorbell of an elderly individual living alone as though he had a package to deliver. His deliverable, however, is a five-minute check-in conversation with a gentleman who might otherwise not talk to anybody face-to-face for weeks at a time. The carrier says that this practice gives him a "happy reason" to walk briskly: freeing up as much time as possible for the visit.
- A desk worker at CVS Health doesn't let anybody in her office experience a birthday or a death in the family without handing them a card from the entire team.
- A worker at a U.S. manufacturing plant invites every new hire to coffee during their first week of employment.
- A receptionist at a veterinary practice prints a book of staff suggestions for grieving the loss of a pet and gives a dedicated copy to clients experiencing that sorrow.
- An outdoor worker at a ski resort sees a "buy one, get one free" deal on gloves, buys a pair for himself and gives the extra pair to a teammate with worn-out gloves.
- A manager makes it a point to learn and remember the names of the custodial staff.

- On snowy days, members of the accounting team at a large company take a break at 3:00 p.m. to clean the snow off the cars in the employee lot. They call it their "winter recess."

- A music composer and pianist who sells music to other musicians has this statement on his website: "Going through a tough patch? Let me know how I can help you play keyboards or compose music. Pay later. Offer what you can afford. Pay with avocados. But whatever you do, keep up your music!" This musician says his most uplifting customer conversations are with grateful customers who take him up on this payment flexibility.

- A manager makes it a point to thank each of his team members each week for a valuable contribution they made.

Remember Verena from Nokia? She was so overcome by the effect of giving someone a choice of a sweet and a bit of attention that she made it her career. She has left her job to become the "Chocolate Angel." Employers hire her to roam the workplace and share edible treats, an inviting smile and an ear. Kindness is so powerful that it's worth

Any gift that comes from the heart, no matter how small, brightens life.

-The Chocolate Angel

investing in. I asked the Chocolate Angel, "How could a small treat mean so much?" She responded, "Any gift that comes from the heart, no matter how small, brightens life."

Job Purposing Method 5: Give Space to a Cause

I'm in a restaurant's back hallway flanked by super-sized cans of corn. I make my pitch to Jerry, the general manager of the family-owned restaurant, "We need to buy supplies and hire a service to haul the rubbish. Can you help?" It's my not-terribly-inspiring attempt to raise funds for the streambed cleanup I'm organizing for a watershed-protection association.

Jerry answers, "No, we won't donate cash." I'm about to thank him for his time and leave when he adds, "I have something better—200 square inches of it," and holds up a paper placemat. It features a large picture of him and a dozen family members spanning several generations and a few paragraphs on the restaurant's history. Jerry explains, "We get the same customers week after week. Now and then they deserve to see something more compelling than me and my family."

Jerry donated the space on 5,000 placemats. We populated it with a black and white photo of a local stream and an invitation to volunteer at the cleanup. The special run was placed in front of every diner for five weeks and raised enough cash to fund my cleanup plus two tree-planting events and added over thirty members to the association, one of whom eventually became a board member.

Like Jerry, we can leverage whatever space our workplaces have to promote social purpose. The following are some of my favorite examples.

- A publisher replaces white space on its letterhead with the logos of its nonprofit partners. Yes, I'm referring to the publisher of this book, Morgan James. And, yes, this practice is a key reason I chose to work with them.

- When the racial-justice protests erupted in 2020, FedEx showed support for the movement by stripping the NASCAR car it sponsored of the purple and orange FedEx paint job and painting the car in the colors and brand of the National Civil Rights Museum in Memphis.

- The IKEA store in Catania, Italy, brings stray dogs into its display rooms. Dogs snooze on the carpets, employees are happy to care for them and customers are charmed by their furry presence.

- A manager of a cavernous train station invites local artists and small businesses to set up inside the station and receive exposure they could not afford to buy.

- TOMS Shoes prints a monarch-butterfly pattern on a line of loafers to build support for saving this species from extinction and uses proceeds from the sales for this purpose.

- An auto-parts store at a busy intersection in a quiet town allows high-school sports teams, the local fire station and other nonprofits use its parking lot for car-wash fundraisers.

- A commercial landlord offers her vacant properties to a nonprofit that uses them as staging areas for month-long neighborhood cleanups.

- Aetna in Hartford, Connecticut, turned its rooftop into a garden that purifies the air and helps reduce the ambient temperature.

- A company's learning and development department offers unfilled seats in its leadership training to staff from local nonprofits.

- Burton, a company that produces snowboards, replaced the content on its e-commerce website with a pitch for the environment during the 2019 Global Climate Strike. Would-be shoppers were redirected to the strike's home page.

The above examples represent a sliver of the possible ways to give space to a cause. We can also use floors, elevators, sides of buildings, backs of chairs, bathroom mirrors, cubicle dividers, keycards and presentation cards to do good.

Job Purposing Method 6: Practice Environmental Sustainability

A young woman has waited in line for twenty-five minutes to talk to me following a presentation I just gave. She introduces herself, "I'm Tina, known as TP Tina, an administrative assistant at a regional trucking company no one has ever heard of." Everyone who preceded Tina in line made a specific request within a couple of minutes. "Can you send the survey you used with HP?" (Happy to.) "Would you be available to speak in Madrid in June?" (Of course!) "What hair products do you use?" (Really?) Tina, on the other hand, tells me a story. About six months earlier, she noticed that her company's janitorial staff threw out and replaced toilet-paper rolls before they were fully depleted (this prevents any stall from running out). Having perfectly good product go into the landfill upset her. She, therefore, asked the janitors to drop the partially used rolls at her desk. Once a week, she delivers the paper products to a homeless shelter on her commute home. Her actions reduce solid waste and allow the shelter to redirect what it previously spent on toilet paper to a monthly ice-cream social for residents. The reason Tina is telling me this instead of enjoying the cocktail party fifty feet away is to gently admonish me. "If supervisors give us junior staff a little direction and autonomy, we'll figure out how to do good from our jobs...and we would love to," she says. I deserve Tina's friendly correction. The presentation I just gave covered only how *managers* could job purpose.

If supervisors give us junior staff a little direction and autonomy, we'll figure out how to do good from our jobs... and we would love to.

-Tina

Tina inspired me to explore the feasibility of *any* worker purposing their own job. I now know she was right—many non-managers job purpose. I've also learned that adopting environmentally sustainable practices is a particularly feasible way for employees with limited authority to start job purposing. Workers all over the world are taking stairs instead of elevators, refusing to purchase items in single-use plastics, bringing reusable beverage containers to work, turning the sink faucet off while they soap their hands and encouraging their coworkers to do the same. What's more, most employers welcome workplace environmental sustainability efforts as they tend to reduce operating costs. Whether we are at the top or bottom of our organizational chart, we can do good for the planet, as the following examples illustrate.

- On learning the art on the walls of the building his firm was about to vacate would be thrown in the trash, an employee organized an art auction that raised thousands of dollars for three local nonprofits and kept dozens of items out of the landfill.

- One administrative assistant set up an office "green jar." Every time someone left their office lights on overnight, they were fined five euros. Proceeds were donated to an environmental nonprofit.
- When a computer programmer needs to clear his head, he straps on rubber gloves, grabs a trash bag and a trash gator, walks out of his office building and collects litter.
- Microsoft charges its departments fifteen dollars per metric ton of carbon they emit, encouraging carbon reduction through budgeting. The money raised is invested in the company's sustainability efforts.
- A cafeteria manager enrolls his team in meatless Mondays. Because meat-based meals consume more water than vegetarian meals, this reduces the cafeteria's weekly amount of water consumed by the equivalent of 1,000 bathtubs.
- Adidas has a line of sneakers and other garments made mostly from plastic collected from beaches and coastal communities, thus reducing the amount of plastic pollution in our oceans.

In summary, workplace opportunities to protect and restore nature abound and are a potent way to job purpose.

Job Purposing Method 7: Develop a Social-Purpose Competency

I have the privilege of advising the leadership of Caesars Entertainment, a company of more than fifty casino and hotel properties. Because resorts and hotels can inadvertently harbor sex trafficking, Caesars' executives saw the opportunity to help alleviate this global calamity in which children and adults of all genders are forced to engage in sex for commercial purposes. Caesars started by training security staff on the tragic circumstances of victims of sex trafficking, how to detect sex trafficking and what to do about it. I helped collect data showing that the training increases sense of purpose at work by 33 percent. One supervisor said that the training, "Not only made me a crusader against this ghastly problem, but also created the part of my job I'm least willing to give up."

Developing a social-purpose skill, as Caesars employees are doing, is another way to job purpose. The following are other examples of this kind of job purposing.

- After several clients drop clues that they are victims of domestic violence, a hairdresser trains to become victim advocate and now knows she is offering the type of support most likely to help.

- A physical education teacher gets certified in adaptive physical education to better serve children with disabilities.

- A flight attendant who feels helpless around autistic youth attends training on assisting families with special-needs children. He's now confident he can comfort children who struggle with travel.

- After seeing automated external defibrillators (AEDs) appear throughout her building, a mid-level manager brings onsite trainers from the American Red Cross to train and certify interested staff in AED use.

- The outdoor apparel company Patagonia offers employees free civil-disobedience training to encourage their participation in environmental protests.

These are merely a few of the ways to job purpose by developing specialized skills. Even learning how to jump-start a car battery or become a more intentional listener, better positions us to contribute.

Job Purposing Method 8: Support the Social-Purpose Efforts of Others

A few months after Michelle Obama became the first lady of the United States in 2009, she agreed to give George Washington University's 2010 commencement speech. But there was a catch. She would only do it if the students, staff, faculty and members of the Board of Trustees completed 100,000 volunteer hours during the school year.

GW medical students ran their own clinic in a blighted neighborhood; staff and faculty revamped the athletic facilities of a school in a low-income community; undergraduates spent their winter break helping Sudanese refugees relocate in Tennessee; and the GW community otherwise rallied to meet the first lady's challenge. She gave them an upbeat commencement speech on May 16, 2010.

Encouraging, supporting and celebrating the social-purpose efforts of others, as Obama did, is also job purposing. Other examples include:

- If a Patagonia employee is arrested at an environmental protest, the company posts bail and provides paid leave for court appearances and other defense-related activities (provided the employee attended the civil disobedience training cited above).
- Alaska Airlines plants a tree for every passenger who brings a pre-filled reusable water bottle onto a flight and posts their action on social media, thus reducing the use of plastic cups.
- A manager invites meeting participants to introduce themselves by sharing what charity they like and why. Not only do

participants learn meaningful things about their colleagues, they provide free publicity to charitable causes and nudge the workplace conversation toward social purpose.

- An art-school director promotes civic involvement by offering a free class to anyone who voted.

- An internal auditor replaces her usual pleas for the audited team to provide the requested data within two weeks with a charitable incentive. If the team submits all the requested information on time, it will receive a charitable donation card to direct $300 to the nonprofit of its choice.

- The CEO at a twelve-person marketing firm asks his team to select one nonprofit to support with a marketing campaign every holiday season. Staff members receive their salary, as always, but the firm does not charge the nonprofit.

- A member of the maintenance department at an office building creates a series of videos to help employees reduce their environmental impact.

- Levi Strauss & Co., which uses the previously mentioned clothing tag that includes instructions on donating the garment, also offers customers a prepaid mailing label addressed to a Goodwill donation center.

- The Walt Disney Company's "Give a Day, Get a Disney Day" promotion provided free admission to its theme parks for individuals who volunteered for at least one day.

Having spent over twenty years helping others make social-purpose contributions, I can attest that supporting the social-purpose efforts of others, as in the above examples, is at least as fulfilling as doing the direct service ourselves.

Job Purposing Method 9: Promote Equity

I'm a ski patroller halfway up a mountain attending Dave, a man in his forties with a freshly injured knee. As I position Dave in the sled that I will transport down to the clinic, he screams obscenities. My offense is being a young woman. He says, "My life is in the hands of a [bleep]ing chick! [Bleep] me!" In between bursts of profanity, Dave laments that the injury might put a permanent end to his skiing (his knee had been surgically repaired twice). I vacillate between anger and empathy for him.

During one of my swings toward empathy, I say, "Dave, if you have to give up skiing, you still might be able to snowboard. Many people with compromised knees do." This only further enrages him.

"Oh Christ! You think I'm going to listen to what a chick has to say about sports? [Bleep]ing unbelievable," he says.

I whisper to the male, and more experienced, patroller who is assisting me, "Tom, since Dave is uncomfortable with me skiing the sled down, should you do it instead?"

Tom responds in a voice loud enough for Dave to hear, "On the contrary. Dave's objections are baseless. Your competent sled running might help him develop proper respect for women." Except for nodding and shaking his head in response to my triage questions, Dave says nothing as I secure him to the sled and take him to the clinic at the base of the mountain.

One afternoon during the following winter, I enter ski patrol headquarters to find Dave waiting for me. He's wearing two things he wasn't when I first met him: snowboard boots and a smile. Dave hands me a box of chocolates the size of a large pizza and says, "Thank you for safely bringing me down the mountain." We talk for about ten minutes. He tells me, "You were right, I can snowboard despite my weak knees. I love it." Eventually, he apologizes for having said "sexist stuff." He seems genuinely sorry.

Sadly, everyday people are victims of prejudice, violence, lack of access and other forms of injustice because of their gender, race, country of origin, religion, sexual orientation, age, mental illness, physical limitations and countless other factors. Like Tom, we can counter these injustices. The following are examples of job purposing that promote diversity, inclusion, accessibility and other equitable treatment.

- A group of programmers modifies the online game their company produces to better serve individuals who are visually impaired.
- A research and development team designs a wheelchair for uneven terrain that allows individuals with low mobility to enjoy the outdoors.
- Starbucks, Walmart and other employers don't ask for criminal history in their job applications to ensure their selection process doesn't discriminate against former felons. (These employers conduct the criminal background at a later point in the hiring process that allows candidates to explain any questionable history.)
- A department manager asks his team members to take an online unconscious-bias training to help identify patterns of discriminatory thinking and reduce biased behaviors.
- One of the most widely respected managers I know consistently asks those who are quiet in meetings to share their thoughts. Not only is this an inherently equitable practice, because there is evidence that quiet participants are disproportionately women and minorities, it counters gender and racial inequality.[67]
- A catering business orders at least 20 percent of its food from small businesses run by women and minorities.
- A line worker at a manufacturing plant adopts a no-racism policy in his conversations. If a coworker belittles Chinese

workers or any other group, he says, "I don't want to be part of conversations that put groups of people down." If this doesn't stop the racist comments, he simply leaves the conversation.

In other words, whether we run our companies or are a small cog in its machinery, our workplaces offer ample opportunities to combat inequity and injustice.

Job Purposing Method 10: Join the Everyday History Makers

I'm sitting across from Jan Jones Blackhurst, a corporate board member at Caesars Entertainment. Her long blond hair and cream-colored jacket trimmed in leopard print are a welcome contrast to the grey-haired men in dark clothing who flank her. She's used to standing out. She has ridden a horse down the streets of Las Vegas while serving as its two-term mayor, has stood on many podiums accepting a variety of awards and has an elementary school named after her. Simply put, Jan is a successful political and business leader who is unafraid to attract attention.

But Jan is the first to clarify that her success has hinged less on standing *out* from others and more on standing *with* others. For example, as mayor in the 1990s, she buoyed the early LGBTQ movement by being the first elected official in Las Vegas to join a gay-pride parade. Similarly, when Jan helped to push equal-pay legislation in Nevada, she started by strengthening existing groups already advocating for this law.

Workplaces almost always include opportunities to support existing social-purpose efforts. This is another way to job purpose. Our coworkers might have already organized marches to demand reform, opportunities to plant trees or meetings to discuss making the corporate culture more comfortable for newly hired military veterans. Examples of job purposing by joining those who are already pursuing social purpose include:

- A heterosexual manager with two gay team members joins the company's LGBTQ employee resource group as an ally to the cause.
- Millions of employees worldwide, at this very moment, are packing backpacks with school supplies for underprivileged students, reading and recording newspaper articles for visually impaired individuals or participating in other company-organized volunteer events.
- A data-entry technician offers to help organize his company's annual giving campaign.
- A manager at a food-services company invites her all-female team of three to start a women's resource group for the entire company.
- Dozens of Walmart employees join an employee-organized walkout protesting the company's sale of guns.
- Two teleworking technical-support specialists write blog posts for their company's public website directing readers to a different digital social-purpose campaign every week.

From a history-making perspective, those who pioneer social-purpose efforts and those who stand with the pioneers are equally important.

-Jan Jones Blackhurst

Joining existing social-purpose efforts is a powerful way for all of us to do good. As Jan put it, "From a history-making perspective, those who pioneer social-purpose efforts and those who stand with the pioneers are equally important."

Job Purposing Method 11: Define the Company or Department as a Social-Purpose Enterprise

In 1973, Ray Anderson founded what would become one of the world's largest carpet and tile companies, Interface. In 1994, Anderson started reading about environmental issues and was horrified to discover that his company was continually damaging the environment. In response, he redefined Interface as a "restorative" enterprise with the new social-purpose charge of helping "customers create beautiful interior spaces which positively impact the people who use them and our planet."[68] The company revised every process in an attempt to have zero harm on nature.[69]

Since 1994, Interface has reduced its landfill waste by 92 percent, its global greenhouse gas emissions by 96 percent and its use of non-renewable energy in the United States and Europe by 99 percent. Anderson died in 2011, but Interface continues on the social-purpose path he set. Several years after the death of its founder, the company announced its new aim of helping to *reverse* the global climate crisis.

For those with proper authority, job purposing can take the form of defining the mission, vision, values, policies or practices of the company or department to be about social purpose, as Interface did. Another example, presented in chapter three, is General Motors' updating its mission to "Zero crashes. Zero emissions. Zero congestion." Other examples follow.

- Ben Kneppers, David Stover and Kevin Ahearn founded a company, Burneo, that collects fishing-net litter from the oceans and refashions it into skateboards, sunglasses and other products.

- Blake Mycoskie founded TOMS Shoes with a commitment to donate a pair of shoes to a child in need for every pair it sold, creating what is known as the "one-for-one" business model that dozens of other companies apply.

- The GiftAMeal app charges restaurants to be featured in its directory. When a user takes a photo at a partner restaurant, GiftAMeal donates a meal to a local charity. If the user also posts the photo on social media, GiftAMeal donates a second meal.

- A solo entrepreneur who provides administrative support to organizations chooses clients who are committed to making a positive societal impact. By supporting only social-purpose enterprises, her everyday bookkeeping helps brighten the world.

- A vice president of procurement at a small office-supply manufacturer decides to transition its supply chain to only include environmentally sustainable products.

- Tesla, the electric-car manufacturer, allows competitors to use its patented technology in the hopes that this will advance the global adoption of eco-friendly vehicles.

If it isn't feasible to redefine an entire enterprise or department, as these individuals have done, it is possible to job purpose by helping just a few individuals, as my next story illustrates.

Job Purposing Method 12: Help Others Develop Their Careers

I'm twenty-nine years old and have recently submitted a bid for a research contract with a Maryland municipality. The county is planning to build a recreation center for a low-income community. It needs someone to conduct a neighborhood survey on the needs and interests of residents, analyze the data and write a report that will inform the design of the center. My chances of winning the bid are low. I'm a solo entrepreneur with limited experience up against several venerable research institutions. To my surprise, the county awards me the contract. As much as I enjoy data analysis, I'm even more excited about a twist I included in my proposal that amounts to job purposing, although it will be years before I invent the term.

I plan to hire local high-school students to conduct the door-to-door interviews after training them in elemental interview techniques and essential workplace skills (such as punctuality, note taking and appropriate dress). My hope is that the project will serve as job preparation for these underprivileged youth.

I hold my first training session with fifteen students. It's a comical scene as we're at the local elementary school and look like giants in the child-sized chairs. At first, I think that's why my young hires look uncomfortable. But after they giggle nervously during their practice interviews, I realize they lack confidence about their ability to do the job. I start second-guessing my decision to hire teenagers. After all, I'm getting paid to deliver results and not to prepare youth for future work. Will these awkward adolescents be able to collect the data? Will they even show up for the next training? As it turns out, nine interviewers attend all three training sessions, set off to ring doorbells and complete the needed interviews.

Doing our work in a manner that supports the professional development or career progression of others, as I did in my Maryland project, is job purposing. It can take many forms and help people of all ages and backgrounds, as seen by the following examples:

- Employees sign up as mentors or sponsors of junior coworkers through formal programs offered by their employers.

- The design team at an apparel company hires underprivileged high-school students as summer interns to expose them to career opportunities in fashion and inspire them to go to college.
- A senior partner at an architecture firm holds a monthly lunchtime pizza party open to any employee seeking his career advice.
- A warehouse supervisor invites non-native English speakers at his company to show up one hour early for their shifts two days a week for free English-language instruction, coffee and donuts.
- The Chobani Incubator, a program named after the yogurt company that established and runs it, gives entrepreneurs grants, resources, mentorship and other support to develop successful natural-food businesses.

This completes the dozen job-purposing methods. However, I've made it a baker's dozen and added one more.

Job Purposing Method 13: Go Beyond the Above Methods

I had a second job-purposing idea for my Maryland research project. I wanted to reward the urban youth with a project-completion celebration at a state park. As someone who revels in serenity when snowboarding in the mountains and hiking in the forest, I considered exposing youth to wilderness a meaningful societal contribution. Others disagreed.

One interviewer's mother, a statuesque woman with dreadlocks, reacts to my field-trip idea with, "Why travel for a bunch of trees and bugs? There's nature right here!" and points to the tennis-court-sized patch of yellow grass down the street. This disagreement on whether my field trip is a meaningful contribution is why I offer it as an example. Job purposing can extend beyond the above twelve methods, which were selected for their feasibility, into unconventional or even controversial territory. Remember that if we consider what we do a meaningful contribution to others or to a societal cause, it is job purposing. Here are examples of unconventional job purposing:

- A manager fires an employee after learning via a social-media video that the employee participated in a white-supremacist rally.
- CVS Health stops selling tobacco products in its pharmacies in an effort to promote good health.
- During the COVID-19 pandemic, a hotel in California offers free astrological readings via phone to those who had to cancel their visits.
- A car wash limits its hiring to individuals with autism.
- A health-records reviewer takes a few seconds to pray over some of the heartbreaking cases she reads.

Not everybody would consider firing an employee for exhibiting bigotry outside of work, providing astrological readings, excluding non-autistic individuals from employment or praying to be meaningful societal contributions. In some jurisdictions, several of these acts might even be illegal. Some of us will push boundaries with our job purposing. Others of us will make sure that we don't. Either way, there aren't twelve job-purposing methods. There is an infinite variety of ways to job purpose. We can each define what works for us.

As Best We Can, Wherever We Are, Right Now

I'm eighteen years old, sitting at the dining-room table completing paperwork for my new restaurant job. My father sits down next to me and asks, "Why are you home?" It's a fair question. I studied diligently in high school to get into an Ivy League university and my parents sold the family's beach timeshare to pay for my attendance. Yet, instead of being on a college campus starting my sophomore year, I'm in my parent's house starting a job as a server.

"Uh, I guess I'm here because I got lost," I respond. As far back as middle school, I had planned on my life being significant in the same way both my parent's lives were: by becoming an engineer and building things the world needed. However, after one year of engineering classes, I only know that diagrams of electrical currents and formulas of chemical processes make me nauseous.

"I don't know how I'm going to matter," I add.

"You know that tonight you will pick up pizza from people working in the kitchen doing their best to make a living, correct? You know that you will serve that pizza to people trying to enjoy a few moments together after a long day of work, right?" he asks.

Seeing my blank look, Papi opens the manila folder he always carries, pulls out a yellow pad and snatches the black felt-tip pen from his chest pocket. He draws a horizontal line, labels the far left "earlier," the midpoint "right now" and the far right "later."

"Where are you?" he asks.

Sheepishly, I place my finger on "right now."

Papi clears his throat. "Then why are you talking about *going to* matter? Why not matter as best you can, wherever you are, right now?" he asks. He then draws a cartoon above "now." It's a woman holding a steaming pizza. Her dark oversized eyes and matching hair make it unmistakably me. Despite my dour mood, I chuckle at the bewildered look of my likeness. Later that day, I introduce myself to every member of the restaurant's staff and learn their names. It isn't much of a social-purpose act, but it's what I could dream up at the time.

My elemental job purposing mattered to one person, maybe more. Like many restaurants in Caracas, this one had a class divide between front staff (servers and managers) and kitchen staff. Compared to kitchen staff, the front staff lived in more upscale neighborhoods and earned three times more. By simply treating the kitchen staff like peers, I helped narrow that divide a notch. On my last shift three months later, a cook's assistant by the name of Pedro tells me, "Before you arrived, no front staff had ever offered me a ride to the metro station or shaken my hand. Thanks to you, now they do."

Many of us spend so much time designing the perfect way to contribute that we never get around to contributing. We're not sure what job we'll have in three months, so we don't start job purposing. We're bewildered by the many job-purposing methods but can't find one that suits us. We perpetually have a few details to nail down before we can activate our job-purposing idea. Meanwhile, opportunities to bring a smile to an elderly individual, save a forest from development or otherwise make a difference pass us by. We serve ourselves and others best by implementing whatever imperfect job-purposing idea we can, wherever we are, right now.

Chapter 7

MANAGING THE DIFFICULTIES
AND RISKS OF JOB PURPOSING

*L*ike anything worthwhile, job purposing involves difficulties and risks, both real and imagined. This section is about mitigating and managing these challenges.

In my Maryland household-interview project, I encountered something that is unfortunately commonplace when job purposing: resistance from others. As mentioned previously, the mother of one of the interviewers disliked my idea of a celebratory field trip to a state park. From there, it got worse.

How to Manage Resistance

In the final week of the project, I ask my nine youth interviewers if they plan to attend the field trip. I arrive home, deflated. "The field trip was a stupid idea. Three RSVPed no and six maybe. No one said yes," I lament to Dirk (my husband at the time).

Dirk responds, "They think it's too good to be true. Don't prove them right. Stay the course." I don't fully understand his point, but he's a Harvard-trained licensed clinical counselor specializing in adolescence, the age group of my interviewers. So, I arrange for the bus, buy foot-tall bags of potato chips, expansive trays of cold cuts, a tub of mayonnaise and other picnic fare. I prepare everything for an event that no one signed up for.

On field-trip Saturday, I park my Volvo at the elementary school parking lot at 8:30 a.m. The only people outdoors on this warm morning are a cluster of teenagers lazily throwing a frisbee on the patch of scorched and littered grass the tall mother considered enough nature for anybody. At the 8:45 a.m. meeting time nothing happens. No one shows up for the field trip. Maybe the tall mother is right. The trip is not a true contribution to the community.

At exactly 9:00 a.m., a gleaming blue coach bus turns onto the narrow main thoroughfare. Against the backdrop of the grey 1950s-era duplexes, the shiny bus looks as exotic as a spaceship. People are coming out of their homes to gawk. I hop on this bus. The female driver, a volunteer from the nonprofit that provided the bus, drives around the neighborhood. Desperate for any takers, I broaden the invitation to all residents. I lean out the open door and shout over and over again, "Everybody is invited to a day of picnicking and swimming. For free! Bring a swimsuit, towel and a sweatshirt to the school parking lot at 9:30."

We fill most of the bus. More than forty youth and adults enjoy a day of eating, tossing horseshoes, throwing frisbees, chasing sponge balls and splashing water. Six interviewers come. Most bring family members or friends. Neither the mother who expressed skepticism about the trip nor her interviewer son is among them. However, the entire clump of frisbee-playing teenagers and over 20 other residents unrelated to the interviewers come. Accordingly, I modify my official remarks to thank the entire community, as opposed to only the interviewers and their families, and realize the adjustment is an improvement. After all, almost every household completed an interview.

A few minutes after arriving at the park, a skinny boy wearing orange shorts runs full speed toward the lake. It's Jesse, the 10-year-old brother of one of the female interviewers. He dives into the crystalline water and disappears under the surface for a few seconds. He is wide-eyed when he pops back up with a fistful of sand held high above his head. "Whoa! There's dirt in the pool!" he screams.

The rest of us laugh. An older boy says, "It's a lake, silly!"

Jesse responds, "I'm in a lake? Oh my god! For real? Does it have a Loch Ness monster?" We laugh again. This time he joins us. On the bus home, Jesse keeps boasting to anybody who will listen, "I was down at the bottom of a *lake*!"

My best interviewer, Maya, sits next to me on the ride home, donning a smile and damp hair. She says, "Thank you, Bea. I had so much fun." I ask her why she hadn't planned to come on the trip when I invited her. She confirms Dirk's suspicion. "None of our bosses at the Dairy Queen or Burger King [local employers] do nice stuff for us," she says. She hesitates before continuing, "This day sounded nuts to all of us, even to our parents. Like a scam trip to Disneyland." I ask her if she still thinks I'm nuts. She smiles before she answers, "Totally! But in a good way now." I decide that I'm okay with the label of a good nut. It's essentially the definition of an innovator.

We are more likely to succeed if we understand that we become pioneers the moment we job purpose. Job purposing is an innovation. As such, others might see it as farfetched or silly. They might oppose it. They might think we're nuts. We should try to be compassionate with our detractors, whether they are our superiors, colleagues, customers, spouses or the very people we are trying to serve. They think their response is reasonable. At first, doing good as a standard part of work sounds too good to be true to most of us. Of course, if their objections suggest we aren't helping, as was the case with Alex (the first grader I tutored), then we do need to halt and reevaluate. But if the objections aren't justified, I suggest navigating around them and proceeding with whatever job purposing is possible.

I almost scrapped my project celebration due to resistance from others. Additionally, I had to adjust the original plan, lest nothing at all happen. I'm glad I "stayed the course," as Dirk suggested. Without a finale of neighbors frolicking in a green field, marveling at the blue water and relishing each other, I would not consider my survey project the runaway success I'm now convinced it was.

How to Come Up with Ideas

If we haven't identified a feasible job purposing idea, we shouldn't worry. There's nothing wrong with us. Well, there actually is, but it's the same thing that's wrong with every person on earth. Allow me to explain with a story of a woman in a gorilla costume.

Two research psychologists showed ordinary people a forty-second video of individuals clad in either black or white passing basketballs to each other. They asked viewers to count the number of times the players in white passed the ball. During the video, a woman in a gorilla suit pranced onto center court, beat her chest a few times and pranced off. At the conclusion of the video, 46 percent of viewers had no recollection of the gorilla.[70]

Almost all of us (90 percent) think we would not miss the gorilla, yet the above experiment suggests about half of us are wrong. Even if we're in the attentive minority who notice the gorilla, the study's conclusion applies to us: We miss obvious things all around us all the time. If not large furry creatures, then something else. We pull into the driveway having no memory of getting off the freeway, don't notice our spouse's new haircut or otherwise miss the obvious. Failing to perceive things that fall outside the focus of our thoughts is a universal phenomenon that scientists call "inattentional blindness." We should be grateful we have it. Without this filtering system, the millions of colors, shapes, sounds, words and sensations that assault us every second would fry our brains.

Inattentional blindness might be necessary, but it's also the reason we miss job-purposing opportunities. At our task-oriented workplaces, our heads are down as we update a plan, fill out paperwork or stock inventory, for example. We aren't looking for opportunities to help others or serve a charitable cause. Thankfully, there's a simple fix. When researchers redirect us to look for the gorilla, virtually all of us see it. If we redirect a small portion of our attention every day toward opportunities to contribute, we will see them. Following is a daily exercise that, over a period of two weeks, will help us do just that.

A Daily Practice for Identifying Job-Purposing Opportunities

1. Set a reminder on your smartphone or computer at one arbitrary time during every workday. For example, at 9:15 a.m., 11:21 a.m. or 4:10 p.m. If you can't easily interrupt your work for fifteen minutes, set the reminder for a time outside of work hours but respond to the questions below in relation to your time at work.

2. Put these questions in the reminder:
    * How is the last person I interacted with doing? What might they be thinking or feeling? How might I contribute to this individual's wellbeing?
    * Can I complete the task I'm doing (or last did) in a manner that is more charitable, equitable, environmentally sustainable or otherwise social-purpose oriented?

- Looking back at the last day of work, what opportunities did it contain to apply one or more of the dozen most practical job-purposing methods?
  1. Tilt a task toward social purpose
  2. Help coworkers with their work
  3. Advocate for a cause
  4. Be kinder than necessary
  5. Give space to a cause
  6. Practice environmental sustainability
  7. Develop a social-purpose competency
  8. Support the social-purpose efforts of others
  9. Promote equity
  10. Join the everyday history makers
  11. Define the company or department as a social-purpose enterprise
  12. Help others develop their careers
  13. Go beyond the above methods

3. When the reminder goes off, stop what you're doing and take fifteen minutes to answer the above questions in writing. Don't worry if you don't get to all of the questions. The exercise will still work.

4. When you have a feasible job-purposing idea, try it out!

That's it! It might take several weeks, but the above exercise will almost certainly generate feasible ways to job purpose.

How to Ensure You Don't Get Fired

Job purposing can be considered a way of messing with our jobs. Might it not, therefore, get us in trouble? It's possible but unlikely. As covered earlier, job purposing might elicit resistance from others, including superiors. But guffaws, eye rolls and indifference are typically the worst we need to tolerate.

FedEx did not fire Dawn, the python-patrolling driver. On the contrary, her boss called Dawn a "superstar." Leroy, the parking attendant who alerted car owners of bald tires, got promoted and soon after received a job offer as a receptionist by an individual whose vehicle he routinely parked. He now has shorter hours, higher pay and is learning office management. Mike, the manager at the manufacturing plant who donated ten dollars from his department's budget every day his team had no safety violations, was nominated by his company's public-relations team to be featured in a regional business magazine. It helped that his plant's safety record beat that of the company's other 130 plants three years in a row. (Eventually, other plants adopted similar job-purposed incentives and he lost the advantage he initially enjoyed.) Mike now has a framed magazine article about himself hanging behind his desk.

No worker has ever told me they were fired, demoted or passed up for a promotion due to job purposing. My experience shows that job purposing is more likely to get us promoted than reprimanded. As you know from chapter three, academic research reached the same conclusion. Specifically, managers tend to reward employees who conduct acts of social purpose with raises and promotions.[71] The ending to the Maryland household-survey project is a case in point.

After I present my findings to the committee that hired me, the chairperson reveals why they chose me over my more experienced competitors. She says my proposal rose to the top because of its "innovative charitable elements." In other words, the evidence suggests that job purposing is more likely to accelerate than undermine career success. Nevertheless, to be prudent, we can always ask for approval.

How to Get Supervisor Approval

Many of us will need or want employer approval before job purposing. As an advisor to dozens of companies, I've spent countless hours helping managers see the value of job purposing. Based on these experiences, I have five tips on making a case for job purposing, whether it's to a line supervisor, a board chair or someone in between.

Tips for Making a Compelling Case for Job Purposing

1. **Call It Corporate Social Responsibility**

   Most managers are familiar with corporate social responsibility (CSR), defined as the social-purpose efforts a company voluntarily does (as opposed to being legally bound to do). The classic forms of CSR include adopting policies to reduce environmental impact, issuing grants to nonprofits and hiring underprivileged and underrepresented minorities, for example. Job purposing is also CSR, albeit a relatively novel version of it. Knowing that job purposing is CSR helps managers become comfortable with it.

2. **Have It Benefit Them**

   Our job purposing will be more attractive to superiors if it helps solve one of their problems or otherwise support their success. Luckily, as covered in chapter three, job purposing improves employee motivation, job satisfaction and performance. As we'll see in chapter ten, however, job purposing can also increase employee engagement, teamwork and retention, as well as sales. The strongest case for job purposing positions it as a way to support one or more of these outcomes.

3. **Share Examples of Similar Job Purposing**

   Whatever job purposing we hope to implement, it will be more palatable to superiors if they know others have done it successfully. Examples from this book can help. Examples from competitors or brands our superiors admire are all the better.

4. **Solicit and Manage Objections**

We shouldn't be afraid to proactively ask our superiors, "What concerns you about this job purposing idea?" The content of this book will help us dispel, or at least manage, their objections.

5. **Make It a Test**

Here are the magic words that have successfully closed more of my job-purposing pitches than any others: "If it's not working for you after ten weeks, I will happily shut it down." Superiors are often impressed and relieved that we favor job purposing *only* if it ends up serving them (and it almost certainly will). A pilot test also lowers risk, making it more likely that our superiors will be willing to try job purposing.

These five practices have served me well. However, it's often the third or fourth conversation that succeeds in securing support for job purposing. We shouldn't get discouraged if our first attempts fail. That's commonplace with any innovation. Instead, we can learn, adjust and try again.

How to Ensure We Are Job Purposing for the Right Reasons

I have a confession. Some psychologists say my thesis that job purposing will improve our lives has a flaw. There is evidence that, for an act of social purpose to improve our work and lives in the ways I've touted, we need to do it *without expecting a benefit from it.*[72] If our reason for job purposing is to become more productive, healthy or wealthy, for example, we are essentially pursuing hedonic purpose instead of true social purpose. As covered in section one, hedonic purpose is unlikely to significantly increase our motivation, job satisfaction, health or happiness. I know it sounds like I glossed over a colossal caveat, but please don't throw this book at the wall. It's not as bad as it sounds. In fact, the solution is likely already in place, and we don't need to do a thing. I experienced this spontaneous fix in my twenties while in the Philippines.

I'm on the Filipino island of Panay planting trees for a reforestation project. My original plan had been to put the shovel down and rush to the beach the instant I completed my three weeks of service. Yes, I admit it. I enrolled in this service trip for the free airfare (covered by the nonprofit organizing the project) to an exotic scuba-diving location. Four days past the final day of the service project, however, I'm still digging holes in the blazing sun instead of diving in crystal-blue water. We, a team of about thirty volunteers from all over the world, improperly planted about a tenth of the saplings and doomed them to dying well before becoming majestic trees. I'm replanting the improperly planted trees days after the organizers thanked us with a beautiful ceremony and sent us on our way, or tried to.

If scuba diving was the planned highlight of my trip, why was I forgoing it? I couldn't have articulated it at the time, but the answer is that I discovered something more alluring than scuba diving: contributing to others or a societal cause. It turns out that social-purpose experiences often transform hedonic motivation into social-purpose motivation. All but a handful of my fellow volunteers also worked beyond their obligation.

Why we start job purposing is one thing. Why we continue is another. Thanks to this distinction, it rarely matters that self-serving job purposing does not accrue many of the benefits listed earlier. No matter how it starts, job purposing rarely remains self-serving. Our initial motivation might be career advancement, increased income or getting a date. But then a villager will explain that the tree we just planted might help prevent another mud slide like the one that killed his cousin, a refugee child we tutor will go from solemn to talkative or a customer will tell us that our kind gesture was the best part of her day. Helped by dopamine, serotonin and oxytocin, per the science presented in chapter three, we'll experience the helper's high. Next, we'll start feeling more calm, valuable and meaningful. Suddenly, we'll stop needing job purposing to boost our success or deliver other extrinsic rewards. We'll be drawn toward social purpose in the same inexplicable way we are to a beautiful sunset or fragrant garden. We will have evolved from a focus on hedonic purpose to one on social purpose. Ironically, since we are no longer chasing the extrinsic rewards of job purposing, we will reap them.

I not only experienced this job-purposing autocorrection on a breezy island, but I also witnessed it at a California construction site, a German office building, numerous other worksites and in data I've collected from companies. These data find that 69 percent of workers who started job purposing primarily for hedonic reasons chose to continue primarily for social-purpose reasons.

To reap the benefits of job purposing, we need to have the intention of genuinely contributing to others or a societal cause. However, job purposing for self-oriented reasons is a productive place to start. There appears to be a seven-in-ten likelihood it will awaken our social-purpose motivation. (If we find the problem persists, however, ensuring that our job purposing meets as many as possible of the Drivers of Highly Transformative Job Purposing in chapter eleven will help).

How to Avoid Compassion Fatigue

We each have challenges, so why invite more? Isn't job purposing a recipe for feeling weighed down by the woes of the world? Isn't it a harbinger of pain and misery? I admit that these questions haunted me for several years. I was concerned that job purposing would aggravate the personal hardship experienced by the already burdened workers of the world. It felt cruel to add to their worries. This was my biggest obstacle in sharing job purposing with all workers, as opposed to focusing only on those fortunate enough to have well-paying professional jobs. It turns out that my fear was rooted in misinformation. What's truly cruel is to *withhold* the possibility of job purposing from workers, regardless of their adversities.

To be fair, there is such a thing as "occupational burnout," defined as exhaustion, cynicism and inefficiency due to chronic stress.[73] If the source of the stress is excessive exposure to the suffering of others, that's a specific type of burnout called "compassion fatigue."[74] In extreme cases, compassion fatigue makes us calloused, hopeless, stressed, anxious and incapable of pleasure. Because job purposing directs our attention toward the pain of others, one would expect it to put us at higher risk of compassion fatigue.

As it turns out, the reverse appears to be true. Compassion fatigue has less to do with being compassionate, defined as feeling concern for the suffering of others, and more to do with the distress of not doing anything about it.[75] Compassion fatigue is a misnomer. Our compassion does not run out. What runs out is our tolerance for doing nothing about the hardship of others.

A study on physicians, for example, found that exposure to the suffering of others rarely causes compassion fatigue. The bureaucratic job requirements that *prevent* physicians from addressing the suffering of their patients, on the other hand, does.[76] Similarly, researchers have found that a *lack* of social purpose makes a job more draining.[77] Other studies conducted on telemarketers and sanitation workers found that job purposing protects against compassion fatigue.[78] Finally, when researchers studied whether the frequent exercising of compassion led those in caring professions to die younger than those in other occupations, they discovered the opposite. Those in caring professions live longer.[79] In other words, the evidence suggests that job purposing reduces our risk of compassion fatigue. This aligns with the findings presented in chapter three that job purposing reduces our risk of mental-health ailments.

This is not to belittle the gravity of compassion fatigue. It might be unlikely that job purposing will trigger it, but it is still a possibility. If we suspect we are suffering from this serious ailment, we need to seek professional help. But it makes no sense to refrain from job purposing for fear of compassion fatigue. If anything, we should fear *not* job purposing.

As an active co-chair of the Bill & Melinda Gates Foundation, Melinda Gates stares into the pit of human suffering on many days. Gates had to decline an impoverished African woman's heartbreaking plea, for example. Having given up hope on her ability to offer her children health and happiness, the woman begged Gates to take them. On another day, a young man died from an entirely preventable disease as Gates held his hand.[80] How does Gates, a strong advocate for mental health, suggest we manage heart-wrenching situations like those above? Gates says, "You'll come to see suffering that will break your heart… don't turn away from it; turn toward it."[81]

You'll come to see
suffering that will
break your heart…
don't turn away
from it, turn
toward it.

-Melinda Gates

How to Not Neglect Our Personal Ambitions

To carve out time to write this book, I limited my client work and speaking engagements to forty hours a week. (I know this is technically full-time, but it's a lighter work schedule than I had at the time.) Under this plan, I would complete this book in under three years. That was one of my most laughable forecasts.

One way I job purpose is by offering deeply discounted or free keynotes to nonprofits. The above book plan was barely in place when what had been a trickle of speaking requests turned into a torrent. Week after week, I found myself far from home speaking to audiences instead of writing. Then a local nonprofit, OneOC, launched an innovative effort to help medium and small businesses pursue social purpose. I was inspired to help and thus spent many unpaid hours on that job-purposing project. Social purpose was derailing me from writing a book on social purpose. The irony! Job purposing was also distracting me from other self-oriented interests like developing my drawing skills and building a retirement fund.

By definition, job purposing invests our time, attention and sometimes money in the service of something bigger than our careers and other self-oriented, or hedonic, goals. Progress toward our self-oriented accomplishments might, therefore, slow. Stay with me, though. If we apply two strategies, presented next, our job purposing will not undermine our self-oriented ambitions.

1. **Embrace the Puppy Route**

    I could have ignored the needs around me and had a solid chance of achieving my self-oriented goals on my preferred schedule. This would have been the equivalent of locking myself in a windowless rocket that shot straight to the completion of the book, masterful drawing abilities and adequate retirement savings. The choice I made was more like walking a puppy to my self-oriented goals. The puppy represents my inclination to do good at work. It's what pulled me toward assisting OneOC and giving discounted speeches. It's what extended the time it took me to write this book to over five years.

I'm glad I chose the puppy route. It brought the wonderful staff and board members of OneOC—and of Innovations for Learning, Points of Light, the Renfrew Institute, the Ruddie Memorial Youth Foundation and other nonprofits I helped—into my life. Furthermore, each free and reduced-fee speaking engagement invariably energized me for weeks. Also, the inspiring job-purposing stories and insightful questions from those audience members informed this book. Compared to the rocket route, my puppy path kept me more motivated, was more enjoyable and produced a better book. I also suspect that, consistent with the research presented in chapter three, my social-purpose path helped me maintain good health.

The alternative to the puppy route—zooming from the start to the finish lines in our isolated rocket—is less enjoyable, fulfilling and productive. Achieving our hedonic accomplishments sooner feels great, but typically for only weeks or months. To feel happy again, we need to rocket our way to a new accomplishment, again forgoing the uplifting effects inherent in work that has social purpose. Studies find that after several iterations of such narrow attention to personal accomplishments, we might find we have achieved our goals, but are nevertheless wallowing in chronic dissatisfaction.[82] We are trapped in what psychologists call the "hedonic treadmill." Using imaging technology to look at the reward patterns of the brains of youth, researchers were able to distinguish who sought hedonic rewards and who sought social-purpose rewards. One year later, those oriented toward hedonic rewards suffered an increase in depressive symptoms, while those oriented toward social purpose did not.[83] Professional success that turns us into unhappy beings, as the rocket route often does, can hardly be considered success.

Furthermore, while the rocket route is more productive than the puppy route in the short-term, it appears not to be the case over the long-term. For example, research has uncovered that medical students who take the time to help classmates have lower grades during the early years of medical school than students who focus on their own performance. But, eventually, the helpful students outperform the rocket-riders. They get better grades in the latter years of medical school and have more successful careers.[84]

Job purposing might give us more to do but, as covered in chapter three, it also grants us more motivation, joy and wellness along the way. It increases our capacity to do more. The net effect is typically greater ease in reaching our long-term goals. Caroline Barlerin is an expert in helping workers bring social purpose to their work and has helped tens of thousands

Expanding work toward social purpose doesn't add work to our lives. It adds life to our work.

—Caroline Barlerin

of workers at Eventbrite, HP and Twitter do so. She notes that, "Expanding work toward social purpose doesn't add work to our lives. It adds life to our work."

My first suggestion on how to ensure that job purposing doesn't undermine our hedonic ambitions, then, is to accept and enjoy the puppy-like disruption inherent to job purposing. As soon as I did this, I became happier and more productive. Still, can't too much of a social-purpose orientation—too circuitous a puppy route—derail our dreams and careers? Yes, it's possible. That's why we need to add a second strategy.

2. **Advance Toward Our Personal Ambitions**

    Serge, a communications director at an apparel company, tells me that he and his two direct reports are at my job-purposing presentation because they want to "do something for the environment." He describes his company's environmental practices as "atrocious." His job-purposing idea is to hire an environmental nonprofit to give lunchtime seminars that develop employee interest and skills in environmental sustainability. However, his team needs social-media training to achieve the department's annual goals. Serge's budget can't accommodate both the all-employee seminars on sustainability and his team's social-media training. He's personally more interested in promoting workplace environmentalism than in meeting the goals on his scorecard. But the thirty-two-year-old is also, in his words, "intent on becoming corporate vice president by thirty-five." Therefore, Serge is in a social-purpose versus personal-achievement dilemma.

    What did Serge end up doing? He did it all. His team attended the two-day social-media workshop. As their in-class project, they crafted and ran a company-sponsored social-media campaign to raise funds for the nonprofit that conducts the environmental seminars. The campaign raised enough money to cover four seminars on workplace environmentalism. It also boosted the company's number of social-media followers, one of the scorecard goals they had previously struggled to achieve.

As seen earlier, embracing our puppy-like inclination to job purpose actually helps us achieve our hedonic goals. However, this first strategy does not mean following the puppy anywhere and everywhere. When the puppy heads in the opposite direction of our hedonic goals, we should probably tug it back. Why? Because the second and equally important strategy is to advance toward our hedonic ambitions as we job purpose. Serge did this by meeting his scorecard goals through job purposing.

Following the puppy on a slightly less direct or slower path to our self-oriented goals is usually enriching and productive. Following the puppy on a complete U-turn that distances us from securing the promotion, starting our enterprise or otherwise achieving our self-oriented aspirations, on the other hand, is likely to foster resentment and, ultimately, be unproductive. I experienced this during the first year I tried to write this book. Feeling the need to accept every social-purpose opportunity, I became increasingly frustrated that my writing was stalled, grumpy that I rarely had time to sketch and anxious that I had made very little progress building my savings. Eventually, I learned that I had to turn down the least compelling half of the job-purposing opportunities. It wasn't always easy to decline offers to serve on the board of a worthy nonprofit or to speak at the graduation of a low-income school, but it allowed me to start advancing toward my hedonic goals and restored my sense of contentment. The bottom line is that the most successful job purposing advances our self-oriented ambitions while serving others or a societal cause.

This advice might sound contradictory. Many of us believe that the more personally ambitious we are, the fewer social-purpose acts we do. But that's akin to saying the more humorous we are, the fewer vegetables we eat. Research finds that self-oriented and social-purpose ambitions are distinct from each other. They don't cancel each other out.[85] Wharton professor in organizational psychology and expert in human social-purpose behavior, Adam Grant, explains, "In my studies of what drives people at work, I've consistently found that self-interest and other-interest are completely independent motivations: You can have both of them at the same time."[86]

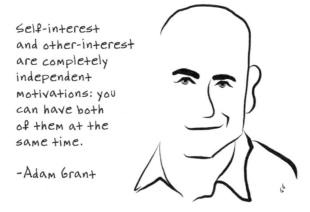

Self-interest and other-interest are completely independent motivations: you can have both of them at the same time.

-Adam Grant

One study that backs Adam's statement is of a group of social-purpose overachievers: honorees of the Caring Canadian Award.[87] These individuals do things like establish a program to help underprivileged girls succeed, share their home with an individual affected by a complex neurological condition and help establish government-funded services for members of indigenous groups with disabilities. Compared to the non-award-winning control group, these social-purpose overachievers have loftier ambitions for their social purpose. That makes sense. They won an award for it. What we might find surprising is that their goodness did not seem to reduce their self-oriented ambitions. The social-purpose overachievers are *more* personally ambitious than the control group that is less interested in social purpose. The social-purpose overachievers aspire to more recognition, power and wealth than the control group. They simply aspire to more all around.

It's telling that many examples of successful job purposing support hedonic pursuits. My free keynotes with nonprofits resulted in corporate representatives in the audience booking me for paid presentations. Furthermore, helping OneOC with its corporate social-purpose efforts connected me to consulting prospects in the Southern California community I had recently moved to. Remember Bill, the hotel conventions director who gave free historical tours? He admitted that this job purposing generates more sales than anything else he does. Similarly, Papi's pedestrian bridge made it more likely locals would welcome the construction project and that his colleagues would consider him a rebellious folk hero, an image he desired.

In summary, our most rewarding and productive career path heads toward our self-oriented ambitions but is enriched with social-purpose experiences along the way.

We're Here for You

The most common challenges to successful job purposing are resistance from others, identifying actionable ideas, ensuring we are doing it for the right reasons, ensuring it doesn't negatively affect our employment, obtaining approval from superiors, minimizing the risk of compassion fatigue and ensuring it doesn't derail our self-oriented ambitions. As covered in this chapter, these challenges are almost always manageable. If, however, you are still having difficulties job purposing, send me an email at HelpMeJobPurpose@BeaBoccalandro.com. I or someone on my team will happily send you customized suggestions free of charge.

Chapter 8

THE RISKS AND COSTS
OF NOT JOB PURPOSING

The middle-aged man wearing crooked tortoiseshell glasses slurs his insults, "What's wrong with you? You ordered an omelet at a steak house. Umph!" He's long known I don't eat meat but won't adjust his choice of restaurant for anybody. I try changing the subject. "I just finished *The General in His Labyrinth* by Gabriel Garcia Marquez. Have you read it?" It's a dumb question. I had forgotten that this frequently inebriated man resorted years earlier to only read, or rather reread, trashy 1970s paperbacks.

Instead of answering, the man sips his gin and tonic. Silence hangs between us like a cold front. "They're imbeciles," he finally says. By "they," he might mean authors, men, Colombians, Nobel laureates or any other group to which Marquez belongs. My lunch date thinks they're all—we're all—idiots. It's his assessment for everybody at some point. I consider walking out midmeal as I did once to this man but decide to stay. This sorry lunch might be the only social event he has all month. He has no friends, no leisure activities (aside from rereading old paperbacks), little disposable income and scarce joy.

The conversation never lightens up. He doesn't congratulate me on my recent engagement, nor does he ask about my siblings. A few minutes later, the man scolds the young waiter, "Are you an imbecile? Did I order burnt steak?" My sternum starts to hurt, a trusted signal that I'm distressed. My eyes tear up.

Who is this ogre, and why am I with him?

He's my father, the formerly beloved Papi. He's the man who MIT professors marveled over, janitors considered a beloved uncle, young engineers admired and most people believed was fated for greatness. What led to his dramatic fall?

It's my opinion that Papi's decline is largely explained by his renouncing the advice he gave his six-year-old daughter: Listen beyond the clamor of your wants for the whisper of the world's needs. To be fair, like all lives gone bad, my father's had multiple troubled threads. He never received the approval he craved from his father, attempted suicide as a teen, suffered an irreparable blow to his dream of becoming a visual artist, developed alcoholism, was robbed of his inheritance by a brother, had an affair that prompted my mom—a magnificent being and the love of his life—to leave him, failed spectacularly as a farmer due to external factors, picked petty fights with his children and sued friends. Identifying which among this long list of factors were causes and which were effects of his downfall is a chicken-and-egg impossibility. We'll never know.

Nevertheless, I believe that Papi's shift in his primary purpose from the wellbeing of others to his monetary interests drove much of his decline. When he stopped following his advice to pursue social purpose, his life diminished just as he would have predicted. It started, understandably enough, over an injustice. In his forties, Papi launched a lemongrass farm and extraction plant in the backcountry of Venezuela. The company's name was Aceites Libertad, or liberty oils, for good reason. I remember Papi's raspy voice explaining that its aromatic oil would transfer income from European buyers of fancy laundry detergent to the plant's nearby dusty indigenous community, Cachama. The production of essential oils would afford the local tribe a pediatrician. But that was merely the beginning of the good my father envisioned. The plant was one step toward creating an agricultural enterprise that would improve lives as far away as Zaraza, a small sun-drenched city 100 miles from his lemongrass fields. In fact, my dad was already pursuing entrepreneurial projects in Zaraza. He job purposed even as he *dreamt up* business ventures.

Papi built a shiny factory on the corner of his vast lemongrass fields but never sold an ounce of essential oil. An energy company drilling nearby extinguished Papi's dream under millions of gallons of spilled viscous petroleum. The spill bankrupted Aceites Libertad, but that wasn't what turned my father into the tragic figure who hobbled joylessly through the last third of his life. I blame his obsession with extracting payment for the damage. A personal lawsuit became his full-time occupation. Instead of working past dinnertime to help Zaraza residents make a living, he did it for his own enrichment. Instead of aiming to bring joy to his team, he wished pain on the "imbecile executives" of the oil company. I still saw glimpses of Papi's social-purpose orientation when he bought whatever homemade product a struggling neighbor sold or bragged about how my public-servant sister did more for impoverished families than the president. But the caustic attitude he displayed at lunch that day was the new norm.

I believe Papi's greatest misfortune was that he started feeling chronically vulnerable to a monstrous corporation and spent all his energy in hedonic pursuits believing he was pursuing justice. For sure, alcoholism, injustice, heartbreak and other misfortunes undermined him. However, like all lives, his always had hardship. Before the lawsuit, he job purposed and was joyful despite difficulties. It wasn't until his focus devolved from social purpose at the top of the Hierarchy of Motivation model to monetary gain at its bottom, per chapter three, that Papi unraveled into a largely inconsequential and bitter man.

Just as we considered the risks of job purposing in the prior section, we also need to consider the risks of *not* job purposing. A job that is not purposed increases our chances of being afflicted with the opposite of the research-established benefits from chapter three. That is, *not* job purposing is associated with an increased likelihood of:

- Workplace demotivation
- Workplace underperformance
- Job dissatisfaction
- Stress
- Anxiety and other mental-health issues
- Heart disease and other physical maladies
- Social isolation
- Unhappiness
- Career stagnation

Put another way, a job lacking social purpose puts some of our success and wellness at risk. Job purposing also carries risks, but these are milder and more manageable. Deciding to *not* job purpose because of its potential perils is like choosing not to exercise because we might pull a muscle. We would forgo a bounty of broad-ranging rewards and a hefty boost toward our success and wellbeing for fear of temporary setbacks. The more productive alternative is to job purpose in a manner that minimizes the inherent but modest risks discussed in this chapter.

Chapter 9

THE POSSIBILITY OF LYRICISM

I'm at a concert talking to Emily, a new acquaintance with an electric blue scarf that matches her eyes. She says to me, "I'm envious of Douglas. I wish my work created something as lyrical as his music. He has me practically in tears." She's referring to the composer playing the piano at the front of the room. I know what she means. Because I'm married to him, my homelife is scored with hauntingly beautiful tunes. Just a few days ago, his playing made me cry into a cup of tea. I wonder the same thing. Could my work, and that of other non-artists, ever be that lyrical?

I pull out my phone to look up the definition. Lyricism is creating something "in an imaginative and beautiful way," per the *Oxford Dictionary*. It applies only to "literature, art or music." I ask Emily if her work involves any of those fields. When she tells me she's a customer-service manager for a cosmetics company, I say, "Well, you and I are both out of luck. Only artists can be lyrical per the very definition of the term." She sighs and agrees that she has never heard of a lyrical middle manager. We both laugh. A few minutes later, Emily leaves and our conversation ends. I, however, can't stop thinking about lyricism. The conversation upset me and I can't pinpoint why.

The following day, on a chairlift while snowboarding, I suddenly know why I'm angry. A world-renowned dictionary, and thus society, insists that my father's work was not and could not be lyrical. With all due respect to the *Oxford Dictionary,* Papi wasn't creating art but his work was nevertheless "imaginative and beautiful." I've known this since I was an eleven-year-old accompanying him on errands.

I'm sitting in the passenger seat of Papi's pickup truck as he drives across Caracas. He's chain-smoking and telling improbable stories. I ask him, "Papi, did that man you know really ride his horse all the way from Zaraza to Cape Horn?" (Zaraza is the Venezuelan city near where my father had several agricultural projects. It is 5,000 miles from the southern tip of South America, Cape Horn.) Papi delighted in telling stories that started in reality and morphed into fantasy. My futile attempts to uncover the truth, assuming there was any, only delighted him further. "No. Of course he didn't ride his horse from Zaraza to Chile! That wouldn't be fair," he says. Papi then clears his throat and continues, "They took turns. The horse rode the man part of the way."

I'm giggling as my dad pulls into the garage of his former employer, the Venezuelan Ministry of Transportation. He's dropping off an envelope. Being a shy preteen, I ask if I can stay in the truck. Papi agrees, leaves and within a minute returns with Marcos, the handyman who told me the story a few years earlier about my dad helping him clean up a spill. Papi wishes Marcos luck getting me to talk, gives me a wink and leaves.

I pull out my book about a teenager who sails around the world solo. Marcos walks to my open window and says, "Just like your dad!" He's right. Papi always carried a paperback in the back pocket of his khaki pants. He would read in waiting rooms, at red lights and anywhere else he discovered an idle moment.

My shyness is so extreme that I barely manage to mumble a soft "yep." Too timid to do anything else, I pretend to read. Marcos steps away from the truck and asks a young attendant to bring him something. The attendant returns with a cardboard box that, per the label, at one time contained reams of paper. Marcos puts the box down on the ground, rummages through a couple of tee shirts, packets of sugar, pens and stuffed animals. He pulls out a small paperback book and explains that the staff threw it in the trash when they cleaned out Papi's office. Marcos then says that he would like to give it to me as I obviously like books and it had belonged to my father. He adds that he "can't do much of that reading thing" and that it's in English anyway. He hands me the book using both hands as though it were a fragile crystal. The book's cover has a drawing of a smiling man sitting behind an enormous desk. It's a manual for engineering software that my sixth-grade brain can't possibly understand. Even as a self-absorbed kid, I am moved by the sincerity of the gesture and barely manage to fight back tears. When I thank him, he responds that this gift can't compare to what my father gave him.

Marcos tells me another story. When Papi was a director at the Ministry, he invited several blue-collar laborers to the department dining room. According to Marcos, the government's food-services director chastised my dad. The dining room was meant only for managers and above. After food services stymied several of my dad's attempts to open the dining room to all workers, he found a loophole. My dad couldn't control who the swanky eatery allowed through its doors, but he could shut it down. So he did. Papi replaced the exclusive restaurant featuring white-linen rounds with an inclusive game room featuring rectangular ping-pong tables. Marcos and his colleagues used it often. "Your dad is an excellent ping-pong player! He beat me many times," Marcos happily exclaims. He then places both hands on his chest and says that, although a subsequent director shut down the game room, no one can take away "the feeling of being as good as anyone else" that my father gave him.

I'm no longer fighting back tears. They are streaming down my face and splattering onto the photo of a sailboat on my book cover.

Papi's work was lyrical. Helping a team member discover dignity in their work or making it possible for an impoverished mother to take her toddler to the beach is as likely to elicit tears or goosebumps as gazing at the Mona Lisa. Scientists have documented it. Just like experiencing art, witnessing an act of social purpose makes us feel inspired, uplifted, warm in the chest, lumpy in the throat and hopeful for humanity.[88] New York University psychologist Jonathan Haidt named this phenomenon "elevation." It sounds like lyricism to me.

Artists are imaginative creators of beauty because they infuse their soaring melodies or muted colors with their heartbreak and hopes. When those of us in more pragmatic jobs allow heartbreak and hope to shape our work, we are also imaginative creators of beauty. If we aren't yet as lyrical with a computer as musicians are with a piano, it's only because we don't job purpose enough. We aren't doing what Papi did, when at his best. His work was unquestionably lyrical and ours can be as well.

III. MANAGING:
JOB PURPOSING FOR
TEAMS AND ORGANIZATIONS

Chapter 10

THE BUSINESS BENEFITS
OF JOB PURPOSING

*K*enneth Cole, co-founder and executive chairperson of the apparel company Kenneth Cole Productions, realized back in the 1980s that he had a problem. He was selling pricey shoes. How could he, in good conscience, ask his employees to work hard (or at all) and be happy about it? Their labor was merely adding shoes to the walk-in closets of well-off people. He described his problem as, "I needed to make what I was doing more important than it was in the ordinary course."[89]

Whether they know it or not, most managers have the same problem Cole had. The ordinary course of business is not sufficiently meaningful for employees to happily exert their best effort. The exception is managers in the nonprofit sector, where work tends to be inherently job purposed. They are lucky enough to manage unusually dedicated and satisfied team members. Research finds that 93 percent of U.S. nonprofit employees work harder than their jobs require, which is triple the national average across all jobs.[90] Similarly, an Australian study found that nonprofit workers are more satisfied than for-profit workers with their work environment, sense of achievement, sense of belonging, level of enjoyment and degree of recognition. That is, nonprofit workers rank higher than for-profit workers on every form of satisfaction measured.[91] No wonder surveys find that 85 percent of U.S. workers who switched from the for-profit to nonprofit sector plan to remain there for the rest of their careers.[92] Nonprofit workers are so cheerfully hardworking that Paul Light, a New York University professor who has studied this group extensively, describes them as living in a "parallel universe."[93] We know where that parallel universe is: at the top of the Hierarchy of Motivation where social purpose resides, per chapter three.

Cole's solution was to job purpose, even if the concept was decades away from formally existing. In the 1980s, for example, the company ran ad campaigns that promoted a compassionate response to AIDS at a time when misinformation on the disease spread freely and prejudice against victims was rampant. The company has done so many AIDS awareness and other social-purpose campaigns that its delighted artists and copywriters don't differentiate between work for Kenneth Cole products and work for societal causes.[94] Did Cole's job purposing solve his problem? If online employee-satisfaction rankings are any indication, it did. The average rating of Kenneth Cole Productions on the Indeed job site puts it among the fifty top-rated workplaces. Kenneth Cole Productions, which is not eligible for the official top-fifty list because it is not publicly traded, has a rating of 4.0. The scores of the top-fifty honorees range from 3.7 to 4.3.[95]

We already know from chapter three that job purposing increases worker motivation, performance and satisfaction. So, unless we have a penchant for apathetic, unproductive and dour workers, we have reason enough to bring job purposing to our teams. Yet, as covered next, the benefits of managerial job purposing extend further.

Job Purposing Improves Recruitment

Three researchers founded a company, HHL Solutions, in order to conduct an experiment. The principal job at HHL was analyzing online photos and entering data for Uber and other companies.[96] When hiring workers for this job, HHL shared information on its social purpose with a randomly selected half of individuals who expressed interest in employment. Specifically, the email that described the position and provided instructions for applying had an additional paragraph about HHL's social purpose:

> "Some of our clients work in the nonprofit sector with various charitable causes. For example, with projects aimed at improving access to education for underprivileged children. We believe that these organizations are making the world a better place and we want to help them in doing so. Due to the charitable nature of their activity, we only charge these clients at cost."

The other half of interested individuals received a "neutral" email with the same details about the job (hours, pay, tasks, etc.) but not the above text on HHL's social purpose. Was the purposed job more attractive to prospects? It was.

The purpose-informed group generated 25 percent more applicants than the neutral group. To attract this many more applicants using pay would have required a 36 percent wage increase. In summary, job purposing is a recruitment tool.

Job Purposing Reduces Turnover and Absenteeism

"I was offered a wonderful job promoting ocean restoration!" my former Georgetown University student, Lisa, tells me. Before I offer my congratulations, she notes, "It would be a 30 percent pay cut, so I doubt I can take it."

Lisa is considering moving from a marketing-director job at a seafood company to the same job at a nonprofit. Studies find that Lisa's experience is commonplace. Moving from a for-profit to a comparable nonprofit position typically entails a pay cut of between 8 and 32 percent.[97] This wage differential confounds economists. Theoretically, for-profits should not have to pay more than nonprofits to fill comparable positions. That's the nature of free-market economics. Why, then, do they? Eventually, economists figured it out. The fancy academic term is "donative-labor hypothesis." I prefer a non-fancy term that means the same thing: bribery. Lisa might keep a for-profit job she doesn't want because, as she puts it, "it just might pay enough for me to tolerate it." That's the definition of bribery: using money to induce someone to do what they don't want to do.

Most of us have at least one Lisa on our teams. We have team members who suffer from knowing their toil doesn't improve a world that troubles them with every unsheltered person or litter-strewn stream they see. They fantasize about a job that makes them proud. I helped conduct research that suggests that on any given day, 37 percent of Fortune 1000 workers entertain thoughts of flight toward social purpose.[98] Other research confirms that employees are more likely to leave their employers if they don't have purposed jobs.[99]

In fact, the news is worse. Researchers find that the team members most likely to leave us because their jobs are devoid of social purpose are our most productive workers.[100] Furthermore, even if a lack of social purpose doesn't cause our workers to leave their jobs altogether, some will partially leave. Research on over 2,000 U.S. workers found that workers who don't have social purpose cut one hour off their workweeks, on average, compared to those who do.[101]

Although her employer offered a raise, Lisa left her comfortable job of many years to work at the nonprofit. Ironically, she chose the switch at the very moment her superiors were celebrating her team's performance with lunch at a high-end restaurant. She explained she was thanked for increasing sales by an unprecedented 23 percent. Yet, the only impact this had on the world was that her employer's competitors sold less. She said, "That's not a reason to stay. That's not a reason to work." She then added, "I can find a way to live cheaply. I can't find a way to keep doing something pointless."

Lisa might not have left the for-profit sector if she had been able to market fish in a way that promoted sustainable fishing or to otherwise pursue social purpose at work. I've helped several companies, including Manulife Financial in Canada and PwC in several countries, collect data indicating that employees without purposed jobs are between 50 and 300 percent more likely to leave their employer than their colleagues with purposed jobs. Remember that Antis Roofing, the construction company with a job-purposed culture, has a turnover rate that is less than one-fifth the industry average. Clearly, team-member retention is another reason to job purpose.

Job Purposing Increases Employee Engagement

As a social-purpose advisor to Caesars Entertainment, I find myself exiting a hotel room at Caesars Palace in Las Vegas. A housekeeper, Luz, is directly outside my door. To collect information on how one of the brand's job-purposing programs is faring, I ask this slender middle-aged woman, "I've heard that you collect partially used soap, is this right?" She reacts as if I had told her that she won the jackpot.

"Yes! Yes! Let me show you!" Luz says. She holds up a translucent bag with two slivers of soap and assures me that it will be full at day's end. She explains, "It's funny, but the soap needs to be washed at a big building." (Caesars helped the nonprofit partner that sterilizes and distributes the soap, Clean the World, build a processing facility in the Las Vegas area.) Luz adds that the soap is packaged "like a birthday present" and sent to families across the country who might otherwise get sick or die because they don't have soap to wash their hands.

Luz starts telling me that a colleague sent her pictures from a company field trip to the plant. As she roots around her phone for the photos, I start feeling antsy. I have a board meeting that I can't be late to. I tell her, "Luz, I need to go, but please text me the photos." I hand her my card and scamper down the hallway.

As I wait for the elevator, I hear the pitter-patter of footsteps. It's Luz. She takes a moment to catch her breath. "I told you the wrong thing! The soap does not go to families all over the country. My company sends the soap to poor families…" With the tip of her fingers, she outlines the largest circle her arms allow and says, "all over the *world*!"

If a company employs more than a few hundred employees, chances are it conducts employee surveys. Typically, the most important survey measure is employee willingness to do more than the job minimally requires, known as "employee engagement." Firms are right to take employee engagement seriously. Gallup finds that companies with high employee engagement outperform their peers with less engaged employees by up to 147 percent in earnings per share.[102] The reality that only 13 percent of workers globally are highly engaged adds to the urgency of promoting employee engagement.[103]

Luz exhibited the signs of a highly engaged worker. She beamed when she talked about work. She went the extra mile—or at least twenty yards to the elevator lobby—to communicate the full greatness of her daily work. She also exuded pride in her employer. I happened to have analyzed the Caesars annual survey data over several years. It shows what

Luz's demeanor suggests: Caesars workers whose jobs are purposed, as Luz's is, have higher employee engagement scores.

Given the plethora of research already presented on the effect social purpose has on worker motivation, performance, satisfaction, recruitment and retention, it should come as no surprise that job purposing boosts the effort our team members put into their jobs. Indeed, one research project I conducted on three companies suggests that job purposing increases employee engagement by 20 percent.[104] A systematic review of all relevant studies corroborates the link between social purpose and engagement.[105] Higher employee engagement is yet another reason to apply job purposing to our teams.

Job Purposing Improves Teamwork and Team Productivity

Job purposing will also reduce uncooperative or uncivil behavior among team members and increase a team's productivity. In one study, researchers divided 500 undergraduate students at a U.S. midwestern university into teams of four.[106] They asked each group to develop recommendations for Gina's Books, an independent bookstore that had experienced a 70 percent decline in revenue over three years.

Researchers gave instructions that emphasized the social-purpose contribution to a random half of the teams: "The store's twenty-five employees…depend on having this job, and many of them have a family to feed…you can make a difference in the lives of the employees of the store." The instructions for the remaining half of the teams emphasized the self-serving aspects of the exercise: "One primary benefit of working on the project is for your consulting team to gain a reputation, which will put you in a position to get consulting contracts with larger companies in the future. This would enable your team to make more money."

Per independent observers who were unaware of the two sets of instructions, the social-purpose groups were less conflictual and more cooperative, kind and forthcoming. They were also higher performing.

The researchers who conducted the above experiment found that the relationship between social purpose and teamwork held true in Chinese and American workplaces across diverse industries and job types.[107] Other researchers have corroborated the above findings and even quantified the job-purposing performance boost in U.S. workers. They found that team members with purposed jobs produced, on average, $9,000 more income for their employer per year.[108]

Job Purposing Boosts Sales

As we learned in chapter three, virtually all humans pine for social purpose. Therefore, we would expect that adjusting the marketing or communications functions to promote a societal cause, as Kenneth Cole's AIDS-awareness campaign did, will attract people to our brands and increase customer loyalty and sales. There is evidence that "cause marketing," as this practice is called, does precisely that.

The personal care brand Dove engages in cause marketing. Specifically, Dove's advertising is designed to help girls develop healthy self-esteem. Its ads feature women as they really are, as opposed to hiring tall and slender supermodels and airbrushing imperfections from their photos. Furthermore, instead of populating the corporate website with traditional sales content, Dove worked with body-image experts to offer tools that build positive body confidence. "Movement for Self-Esteem," as the campaign is called, has delivered self-esteem education to more than 19 million young people across 138 countries.[109]

Research suggests that Dove's self-esteem ads likely have a profound impact on us. Biometric tracking of consumer pulse, facial and skin reactions shows that cause-marketing ads create a deeper visceral connection to a product or brand than those that don't feature social purpose.[110] A social-purpose ad generates the same physiological response that gazing into the eyes of a loved one does. Surveys corroborate these biological findings. Nearly two-thirds of the 30,000 consumers surveyed worldwide prefer to purchase products and services from companies that stand for something meaningful.[111]

Consistent with research findings, Dove's sales increased from $2.5 billion to $4 billion in the first decade of the Movement for Self-Esteem campaign. These results convinced Dove's parent company, Unilever, to expand cause marketing to its more than 400 brands. Commercials for Brook Bond tea, for example, now emphasize overcoming prejudice through teatime conversation. Unilever's social-purpose brands now number twenty-six, including its six largest: Dove, Lipton, Dirt is Good, Rexona, Hellmann's and Knorr. As Unilever expected, the brand migration appears to be paying off: Its social-purpose brands are growing 50 percent faster than its other brands.[112] This finding is not just a Unilever phenomenon. An eight-year study published in the *Harvard Business Review* found that companies that engage in social purpose enjoy higher growth than those that don't.[113] In short, those of us in company leadership, communications or marketing positions can boost sales through a form of job purposing called cause marketing.

The Total Effect: True Leadership

I've already mentioned the sex-trafficking training and soap-recycling programs at Caesars Entertainment. Gwen Migita, Caesars' Global Head of Social Impact, Equity and Sustainability, leads the team that runs these initiatives. Those two efforts would be enough to bestow the label of exceptional leader on soft-spoken Gwen, but her accomplishments go much further. Her programs have earned Caesars several awards, including the 100 Best Corporate Citizens by *Consumer Reports* magazine, the Civic 50 by Points of Light and America's Most Just Companies by JUST Capital and JUST Capital Foundation. One of her team members joked that Gwen's thinking was so far ahead of others that "she might be from the future." Another said, "I marvel at Gwen's quiet genius every time I meet with her." Conference organizers clamor for her to speak. Harvard Business School and Accenture have written up her work.

Gwen's job purposing is a likely driver of her leadership success. Researchers know that leaders who job purpose earn higher status and greater respect.[114] They've also discovered that companies that have social purpose as part of the culture perform 42 percent better than the market.[115] Similarly, a Havas Group study found that companies with widespread job purposing outperform the stock market by over 200 percent.[116] Gwen summarizes all this evidence into what appears to be a new management truth, "Leadership that doesn't improve the world, or at least some sliver of it, can no longer be considered leadership."

Leadership that doesn't improve the world, or at least some sliver of it, can no longer be considered leadership.

-Gwen Migita

Chapter 11

THE DRIVERS OF HIGHLY TRANSFORMATIVE JOB PURPOSING

*L*et's imagine that we manage a team of twenty sales representatives at Noprag, a technology firm afflicted with low employee engagement (meaning employees tend to put little effort into their jobs). One day, we walk into the office lobby and see a wall plastered with a gripping seven-foot-tall photograph. It's of a woman in a vast green field holding a rake who, despite her simple dress and chapped hands, exudes nobility.

The poster's print says that a $750 loan will help Anya, who has a strawberry farm in Tajikistan, buy a greenhouse and pull herself out of poverty. We read further. An online crowdfunding platform gives anyone the opportunity to loan money to Anya and thousands of other low-income entrepreneurs. Noprag is providing each employee with twenty-five dollars for a loan to the entrepreneur of their choice.

Super! Our employer has a solution for our team's low employee engagement. If we encourage our sales representatives to participate in Noprag's microloan program, their employee engagement will naturally increase. However, a few months into the program we learn that measures taken before and after participation, and compared to a control group, show no increase in employee engagement. These are real results from a real program at a real company (Noprag is not its real name). I analyzed the data myself. This particular job purposing did not affect employee engagement, as I claimed it would in the last chapter.

I was so confounded by the lack of relationship between participation in the Noprag microloan program and employee engagement that I assumed I was doing something wrong. I forwarded the data to John Peloza at the University of Kentucky, an expert on the effects social purpose has on workplace behavior, to conduct an independent analysis. His team corroborated my confusing conclusion.

Since then, I've studied the relationship between social purpose and employee engagement, performance, recruitment and retention at CSAA Insurance Group, John Hancock, Orange, PwC, Toyota, Western Digital and more than a dozen other firms. The lessons from these hundreds of thousands of rows of data and from the dozens of studies conducted by others have helped explain the failure of Noprag's program in boosting employee engagement. So, what's the explanation? Is the information I presented earlier on the effect job purposing has on employee engagement wrong? No, it's not wrong. Job purposing *will* increase our team's employee engagement—as well as retention, teamwork and performance—*if it meets certain criteria.*

It turns out that, while the personal benefits of job purposing appear to materialize with just about any act of social purpose, the workplace impact materializes only when the social-purpose acts meet certain conditions. Per the data presented in chapter three, contributing a few dollars or minutes toward social purpose improves our health and happiness. In fact, we are so sensitive to social purpose that merely *thinking* about it positively affects us. For example, a classic Harvard experiment that asked people to watch a one-hour film on charitable behavior found that it improved their immune function (relative to the control group who watched a film on another topic).[117] In other words, almost any quantity and type of job purposing has a positive *personal* impact. As the Noprag case shows, however, not all job purposing has a positive *workplace* impact.

The existing body of knowledge has identified eight Drivers of Highly Transformative Job Purposing that drive the positive effects of job purposing on workplace behavior:

- **W**ork-related
- **E**mployee-crafted
- **G**roup-based
- **I**mpact-evident
- **V**iscerally-meaningful
- **E**volving
- **I**ntrospective
- **T**enderly-led

As you can see, the Drivers are arranged according to my admittedly dorky, but hopefully memorable, acronym: WE GIVE IT. Following are the details.

Driver 1: Work-related

A key reason the Noprag microloan program doesn't boost employee engagement is that it's not woven into actual work. My research, along with that of others, has discovered that the more distant the social-purpose activity is from what employees consider their jobs, the less likely it is to boost employee engagement, retention and other workplace outcomes.[118]

A reasonable indication that a program does not meet Driver 1 is that team members don't talk about their job purposing when asked about work. The Noprag employee survey asked respondents about the "best part" of working there. Some employees submitted comments like "I can't think of anything except leaving at the end of the day." Yet, a few questions earlier they had said, "I love the microloan program. It's so uplifting." They saw their jobs and social-purpose actions as distinct and separate. The microloan program was not true job purposing because it was extracurricular to work. It was like a good vacation. It increased happiness and health but not enthusiasm for writing a brief, wiping down a counter or other work tasks.

An example of job purposing that is tightly linked to work, and thus, aligns well with this Driver comes from HP. This global technology company invites sales staff to attend training on helping business clients become more environmentally sustainable—a competency and commitment that runs deep at HP. Once trained as "Eco Advocates," sales staff can offer prospects assistance in reducing their carbon footprint, energy consumption, solid waste and water use. Staff find that preserving nature and selling HP products are interwoven threads of their standard sales call. They've said things like, "The highlight of my week was that a prospect not only signed a contract with us but is switching to renewable energy." Unlike Noprag employees, HP employees see no separation between their job and their job purposing. Do Eco Advocates have higher levels of employee engagement? I analyzed the data and found they do.

Another example of job purposing that folds into work seamlessly comes from LinkedIn. When work volume is low, call-center employees have the option of calling the donors of LinkedIn's partner nonprofits to thank them for their generosity. Using their phone skills in support of terminally ill children, local artisans or other worthy causes infuses their work with purpose. They also report that expressing gratitude to delighted listeners is a welcome break from their typical problem-solving conversations.

A third example of work-related job purposing comes from Soma Franks, the co-founder and co-owner of Sweetwater Harvest Kitchen in Santa Fe. Soma dislikes paying processing fees to credit card companies. She, therefore, came up with an ingenious way to do less of it. If customers pay in cash, Sweetwater donates 2 percent of their payment to that month's featured local nonprofit. The restaurant accrues the same amount of revenue, customers pay the same amount and local nonprofits are better known and better funded. Of course, this also benefits Sweetwater. Customers have a more positive experience because of their social-purpose act, the Sweetwater brand gets a cause-marketing boost and twelve nonprofits a year encourage their supporters to frequent the restaurant.

In the case of HP, LinkedIn and Sweetwater—as well as Papi's pedestrian bridge, Dawn's python patrolling and Leroy's tire checking from earlier chapters—the social-purpose activity is baked into a core work task, be it selling, talking, billing, designing, driving or parking. Per the first of thirteen ways to job purpose presented in chapter six, such tilting of a core task toward social purpose is the highest-impact method. It makes the job purposing more ubiquitous and, thus, more likely to meaningfully help the societal cause and to improve the employee's relationship to work. It's the gold standard for job purposing. There's just one problem.

Sometimes it's not feasible to do good from the core of the job. So, what's plan B? The next best option is to integrate social purpose into workplace activities that are noncore to the job but still central to the overall work experience. IBM, for example, job purposed its leadership development function through its Corporate Service Corps.

IBM selects top management prospects and then trains and dispatches these budding leaders to developing countries around the world. Groups of ten to fifteen participants spend four weeks onsite helping to solve the economic and social problems of their selected beneficiary organization. For example, a Corporate Service Corps team worked onsite at the Vietnamese Department of Health to help improve its efficiency in patient treatment and disease prevention. Clearly, this is a radically more rewarding way to develop global leadership skills than sitting in a classroom.

Meeting facilitation is another noncore task that we can job purpose. Eileen, a manager at Aetna, led a company committee of over 40 employees that supported her department. She invited committee members to facilitate the monthly calls on a rotating basis. On most months, however, no one volunteered and Eileen found herself running the calls. She then decided to give each meeting facilitator a $150 donation from her department's budget to direct to the nonprofit of their choice. It has been several years since Eileen instituted this practice and she hasn't facilitated a single call since.

In summary, there are many ways to make job purposing work-related. If we can't job purpose the tasks that are core to the job like HP's Eco Advocates program does, we can focus on more sporadic work experiences, such as training, meeting facilitation or team-building workshops. Additionally, any job purposing performed with coworkers typically feels work-related and, thus, meets this Driver. Nevertheless, we shouldn't panic if the best we can do is a solo off-site volunteer experience that is distinct from everyday work. Remember that Yankees ballplayers appeared to get a performance boost from taking children to the zoo, an activity that is distant and unrelated to their job on the baseball diamond. Meeting several of the other seven Drivers is typically enough for job purposing to positively impact workplace behaviors even if this first Driver is not met.

Driver 2: Employee-crafted

"Requiring workers to ask permission to do good at work is absurd and counterproductive." This statement would be easy to dismiss as naive if it weren't from Frances Edmonds, the widely admired leader who founded Eco Advocates, led HP Canada to become one of Canada's greenest employers (per Canada's Top 100 Employers) and was honored as a top sustainability professional by the Clean 50.

Requiring workers
to ask permission
to do good at work
is absurd and
counterproductive.

-Frances Edmonds

I believe that Frances, Head of Sustainable Impact at HP Canada, has detected a shift within capitalism that most of us have missed. With each passing day, it becomes increasingly important for companies to encourage and equip employees to job purpose as they see fit.

No decent manager would require their team members to ask permission before assisting a colleague. We expect employees to routinely help each other learn to use software, create better products or cover a shift. We trust our team members to contribute to colleagues in a way that doesn't undermine their performance, spend excessive company resources or otherwise be counterproductive. Of course, if an employee's service to others depletes the department's budget or adversely affects her own ability to accomplish her work, we help her make adjustments. But we wouldn't introduce a policy that no one should help anybody else learn a PowerPoint feature without first securing approval. Supporting and encouraging natural-occurring employee-to-employee assistance makes sense because employees make up an ecosystem. The healthier the ecosystem, the more successful we are as managers.

Increasingly, employee chatter spills from the breakroom into social media. Their concerns extend beyond the wellbeing of coworkers to that of natural-disaster victims halfway around the world. Customers know, and post online, if a company has polluted oceans or exhibited prejudice. In other words, the new business ecosystem extends to the broader society. Therefore, it is now sensible to entrust our workers to contribute to their new expanded ecosystem without the hindrance of prior approval. As with everything they do, we should expect that their job purposing supports the success of the company or at least doesn't undermine it. If our team members' job purposing fails in this regard, we need to intervene. Nevertheless, giving employees the training, tools and freedom to make their own job-purposing decisions is the new productive norm.

Placing the job-purposing decision in the hands of employees is precisely what Frances does at HP. From its founding, Eco Advocates gave employees a voice in its design and ample flexibility in its application. However, another program that Frances cofounded in collaboration with WWF Canada is an even clearer illustration of empowering employees to craft their own job purposing. In fact, that's the goal of the Living Planet @ Work program. It equips any interested employee with ideas, tools and support to drive environmentally sustainable practices at work. Armed with materials from Living Planet @ Work, employees have created carpooling programs, eliminated single-use plastics in the office and cleaned up neighboring natural areas, for example. Such employee involvement in designing their own job purposing leads them to become more attached to the job purposing. Valuing something more because we helped build it is a known phenomenon that academics call the "IKEA effect" after the Swedish multinational that has customers assemble the furniture they buy.[119]

The Noprag microloan program performs relatively well on this Driver. It gives employees the choice of which entrepreneur to support with the company's twenty-five dollars. This might appear too small a role, but it doesn't take much to trigger the IKEA effect. I suspect that if the Noprag program performed better on another two or three Drivers, it would drive employee engagement. Unfortunately, this is the single Driver it meets to any meaningful degree.

If we can't give our team members the carte blanche that Frances espouses, offering them limited authority in crafting their job purposing still helps. For example, managers have established employee committees to run the job-purposing program's activities, held friendly competitions to name the program or assigned teams to design the program's tee shirt. The point is to have team members play at least a small role in shaping their job purposing.

Driver 3: Group-based

When companies want me to measure the impact their job purposing has on employee engagement, retention and other employee outcomes, I ask them a question: Do employees perform their social-purpose acts *with each other*? If the answer is no, I suggest not measuring the program's impact until they can answer yes.

Based on data from over twenty companies, performing the job purposing with coworkers is the single best design element to boost employee engagement and retention. This is partially because, as mentioned earlier, it automatically makes the experience work-related. That is, meeting Driver 3 is a way to meet also Driver 1. But Driver 3 adds its own value: It strengthens workplace social connections, which in itself increases employee engagement and retention. Whether the job purposing was already work-based or not, making it group-based will almost certainly further augment employee engagement, retention and other desirable workplace behaviors. Previously presented examples of group-based job purposing (from chapter six) include the cafeteria team that offers environmentally friendly meatless Mondays, the marketing-firm CEO who asks his team to select one nonprofit organization to support with a free-of-charge job every fall and the group of programmers who modify their company's gaming products to better serve individuals who are visually impaired.

Sometimes we can mold solo job purposing into a group activity. Participants in Eco Advocates, for example, typically help clients adopt sustainable practices without the presence of coworkers. Other aspects of the program, however, such as webinars, celebrations and online discussion groups make it clear that participants are part of a team. Similarly, a manager who encourages her team members to serve on nonprofit boards can have them train together and meet episodically to support each other's board service. Furthermore, while many companies have volunteer-grant programs in which the company gives a small grant to the nonprofits where individual employees volunteer, Best Buy offers the team version of this program. It gives $500 to nonprofits that benefitted from at least five employees (two at smaller locations) volunteering together. Noprag does not perform well on this Driver, but it easily could. It could offer groups of four or more workers $200 to direct to a micro-entrepreneur of their choice, for example.

In other words, there are many ways to make job purposing a group activity. This is fortunate because the degree to which the job purposing impacts employee engagement, retention and other positive workplace behaviors hinges largely on this one Driver.

Driver 4: Impact-evident

Duke University's Dan Ariely and his team conducted a study in which they paid Harvard students a small amount for each Lego figure they assembled. Students were randomly divided into two groups. Both groups received the same instructions and pay. The only difference was what the experiment organizers did with the completed figures. Members of the first group saw theirs accumulate. The organizers placed each assembled figure in plain view and gave them a box with new Lego pieces to build the next one. On the other hand, the second group witnessed the organizers immediately disassemble their creations and place the pieces back into the box. Hence, their finished work did not accumulate.

The first group worked longer and took home 25 percent more pay.[120] Other studies have similar findings.[121] Being aware that our efforts make an impact, even if it's just creating Lego figures, increases our motivation. The fourth Driver of Highly Transformative Job Purposing, then, is ensuring the workers feel confident their job purposing makes a difference.

The Noprag microloan program is weak on this Driver. The program's impact is not necessarily evident to workers as the benefitting entrepreneurs are distant and their progress is not shared with workers. Eco Advocates has a similar structural challenge. Reducing greenhouse gas emissions and minimizing water use are distant and intangible accomplishments. Nevertheless, business customers routinely thank Eco Advocates for lowering their costs and raising their sustainability. HP employees at least know they positively impacted a customer well beyond expectations. Furthermore, unlike Noprag, HP takes great pains to ensure that employees understand their ultimate effect on the environment by setting and tracking goals and creating dashboards. As a result, HP ends up performing moderately well on this Driver.

If our team members are teaching first graders to read or are otherwise performing social-purpose acts where the impact is inherently evident, there should be little need to do anything additional to meet this Driver. Team members will witness their impact. Most job purposing, however, takes place far from the good it generates. In these cases, we should do what we can to connect the dots between team members' efforts and a positive result. We can create materials that tell the story, as HP does, or we can ask the nonprofit to share a video showing how employee contributions improved lives. Anything that ensures our team members understand their positive impact helps solidify the benefits of job purposing.

Driver 5: Viscerally-meaningful

On my birthday one year, I find myself under the Las Vegas sun repairing and painting a dilapidated wall at an impoverished elementary school. The meetings department of Caesars Entertainment had organized a service project as part of its annual preferred-vendor conference. Caesars employees were at a social-purpose activity alongside the company's most important meetings and conventions clients. My husband, Doug, and I joined in.

I'm finding it enjoyable to fill a large bucket with paint, walk from volunteer to volunteer, refill their trays and chitchat for a minute or two. Then a first-grade student shows up at the school with his mother. The boy's eyes grow large when he sees the freshly painted sky-blue wall. "So pretty!" he shouts. He then runs to the wall, high fives it and runs back to his mother saying "Look, mom! My school is like new!" At that moment, he seems as proud of his modest school as any private-school student ever was of their gleaming campus. That his right palm is blue with wet paint only seems to intensify his giddiness. Suddenly, I no longer find my social-purpose activity pleasing. I find it elating.

Why did witnessing this boy's joy augment my happiness? Jonathan Haidt (the same psychologist who defined the concept of elevation presented in chapter 9) uses an analogy to explain the difference between our thoughts and our emotions. Imagine an elephant and a rider. The rider represents our rational thoughts and the elephant our emotions.[122] The rider in me can direct the elephant in me to fill a tray of paint, for example, and I will dutifully do just that. But if the elephant in me gets joy out of this and thus *wants* to refill a tray of paint, my rider won't have to coax it. The elephant will charge happily toward that tray. All of me will suddenly be fully engaged in the task.

Within a minute of arriving at the school, my brain knew that my service would likely improve the lives of students. That is, the project met Driver 4, or was impact-evident. That realization, however, only spoke to the 100-pound rider, a small part of my psyche. Most of me, the 13,000-pound elephant, was disengaged. The ebullient boy was the visceral message that told the big and emotional part of me what the tidy and logical sliver already knew: My contribution matters to others. Job purposing that is viscerally meaningful, as this school project was to me, is more likely to boost employee engagement and otherwise generate a positive employee response.

An experiment on a group of telemarketers raising funds for scholarships illustrates the power of meaning that is viscerally felt. Fundraisers for a scholarship program who listened to a recipient give a ten-minute in-person talk on the impact the scholarship had on him raised 171 percent more in donations the following month than those who read a letter from beneficiaries with similar information. The magnitude of the increase was so startling that the researcher, Adam Grant (the same Wharton Professor who taught us that self-interest and social purpose do not diminish each other), at first doubted it could be attributed to a simple presentation. Subsequent iterations of the study, however, merely confirmed the first study's finding: Visceral evidence that our efforts help others can dramatically augment our performance.[123] Another study on social-purpose efforts directed at coworkers reached the same conclusion.[124]

Relative to this Driver, HP's job purposing has an advantage over Noprag's. HP team members have direct contact with clients who often express heartfelt gratitude, while Noprag workers only interact with a website. So, while HP does not perform exceptionally well on this Driver, it performs well enough. Noprag, on the other hand, has nothing in place to meet this Driver. The bottom line is that authentic personal expression of the positive impact of job purposing, ideally from beneficiaries, will amplify the resulting boost in performance and other employee outcomes.

Driver 6: Evolving

I'm at a reception in New York talking to Scott, a manager at a financial institution who I had worked with two years earlier. He's updating me on the evening workshops that help low-income individuals claim tax credits that I helped his team develop. "We tried to not change anything you set up, but somehow still messed it up," he says. He explains that team members started losing interest and that he's barely getting enough volunteers to hold the workshops. I understand why he's perplexed. Until a few months ago, his sixteen team members loved these workshops. The majority of them happily attended, gushed in the post-event reflection sessions and brought a palpable positivity to the office that lasted for days.

The problem with Scott's job purposing is the exact opposite of what he thinks. It isn't that he somehow changed something that weakened the program. It's that he didn't change the program frequently enough to maintain his team's interest. Researchers have long known that even wonderful experiences lose their luster with repetition.[125] Our job purposing needs to evolve to remain popular.

Luckily, there's no need for radical overhauls. Research finds that even minor adjustments rekindle our interest in an old experience. For example, experiments find that people who were tired of drawing a photograph drew with sudden gusto when researchers asked them to draw an upside-down version of the same photograph.[126] Equally modest updates to job purposing are enough to restore interest in it.

There is an infinite number of ways to evolve our job purposing in both small and large ways. We can expand social-purpose offerings. Scott's team, for example, ended up adding a barbeque dinner to the workshop. This adjustment attracted team members who loved to grill, added a festive feel to the service project, helped ensure low-income families had a good meal that one day and made the tax-credit workshops a team favorite again. Alternatively, we can broaden participation by, for example, inviting family members or another department to join the job purposing. We can also add a time-limited element as a drive-through coffee shop did. It had long given a 10 percent discount to drivers who shut their engines off instead of idling during the wait or who drove electric cars. On election day, it expanded this positive-behavior discount to drivers who could show evidence of having voted.

The Eco Advocates program meets this Driver by continually adding modules, inviting new groups of employees to participate, expanding whom it helps and otherwise renovating itself. Noprag's microloan program, on the other hand, has hardly changed from one year to the next and participation has dropped accordingly.

In other words, endlessly repeating our successful job purposing does not necessarily result in endless success. We need to refresh our job purposing continually.

Driver 7: Introspective

"To learn what I think, I look back over what I said earlier." We might believe this statement only applies to inebriated party guests and politicians. Yet, Karl Weick, professor of organizational behavior and psychology at the University of Michigan, finds that it applies to all of us.

Weick's contention that we attain a sense of meaning through verbal expression is now widely accepted among psychologists. Meanwhile, educators have reached the parallel conclusion for their field: Verbal reflection after a lesson, be it classroom or experiential, augments learning. Consistent with the findings from these two fields, research finds that reflection augments the happiness boost of workplace social purpose.[127] In other words, talking (or writing) about the job purposing amplifies its positive impacts.

Providing structured opportunities for team members to talk about their job purposing is the seventh Driver of Highly Transformative Job Purposing. Specifically, I suggest inviting workers to share their thoughts on the following three questions.

1. What did you like about the job purposing?
2. What could be improved?
3. What changed or will change for you because of this experience?

This reflection exercise takes only a couple of minutes and can be conducted as infrequently as once a quarter for ongoing job purposing or after each event for episodic job purposing. While it is most effective in person, phone calls, emails, internet surveys and text surveys are reasonably effective alternatives. Eco Advocates, for example, incorporates ongoing reflection using surveys, online forums and occasional in-person meetings. Noprag's program, on the other hand, lacks structured introspection and this likely hinders its success.

In short, structuring reflection into job purposing increases its positive impact.

Driver 8: Tenderly-led

The CEO of Antis Roofing in Southern California, Charles Antis, wears his heart on his sleeve. Specifically, the linings of his custom suits are patterned with the logo of Ronald McDonald House Charities, the organization that provides free housing to the families of children receiving medical treatment away from home. Technically, Charles displays his soft spot for this charitable organization on the *inside* of his sleeves, but my point still stands. Charles is comfortable showing that he cares. I've even witnessed him cry.

Meanwhile, Will Hockney, the Director of Marketing at JACK Entertainment in Cleveland, Ohio, literally opens his door to problems. Team members are invited to walk into his office and share concerns, ideas or whatever else is on their minds. Will's department meetings have the same type of compassionate openness.

Charles and Will exhibit the type of tender management that makes many businesspeople uncomfortable. This unusual approach, however, has worked. They've both led flourishing job-purposing practices that, by all indications, have strengthened the performance of their teams.

One way that Charles job purposes is by rewarding a high-performing team member with a company-branded charitable gift card at staff meetings. The winners direct the twenty-five-dollar donation to the charity of their choice and, at the following staff meeting, are invited to share which cause they helped and why. Recipients talk about the youth mentor who never gave up on them, the hospice team that cared for their dying mother or a societal injustice they wish to vanquish. It's at these presentations that you will catch Charles wiping away tears. In addition to using charity gift cards for recognition, his company roofs every local Habitat for Humanity house free of charge and frequently holds events that support other causes.

Similarly, Will's team members have raised funds to buy a cellphone for a new hire, collected hand-me-down professional wear for another team member and provided the gifts and food that allowed a low-income family to celebrate the holidays. One team member with mechanical skills even does oil changes for his colleagues. Job purposing is routine for Will's team.

As we have come to expect from job purposing, both Charles and Will's teams overperform. *Roofing Contractor* magazine placed Antis on its national list of Top 100 Roofing Companies and *Professional Roofing* magazine named it one of the Top 100 Roofing Contractors in the country. Furthermore, the 100-employee firm single-digit turnover rate is less than one-fifth the industry average.[128] Similarly, Will's department is the top performer in its company's annual engagement survey with an almost-perfect 98 percent overall score. Furthermore, although his team represents less than 1 percent of the property's workforce, it earns over 10 percent of the Employee of the Month honors and was instrumental in the property earning a spot as a Top Workplace from the *Cleveland Plain Dealer*.

When asked why his unorthodox management style works, Charles said, "It takes guts to be vulnerable at work, though it actually makes everything easier." Will answered the same question with "Being open to the needs of coworkers might look like a complication, but it's a positive

It takes guts to be vulnerable at work, though it actually makes everything easier.

-Charles Antis

one." He explains, "Having a happy family requires caring about others. Few of us would forgo family life because of this complication." As will be covered in chapter twelve, anthropologists back him. Three million years of tribal existence encoded into our genes a yearning for family-like connections with the one or two hundred people we see most often. In the modern world, these are most often our work connections.

By broadening the focus of work beyond the tasks of the week to the wellbeing of team members and society, Charles and Will aren't conforming to typical guidance issued by departments of human resources. For example, HR policies often discourage the personal conversations and in-kind donations among employees that Charles and Will encourage. In fact, many job-purposing applications trample on HR guidance. Earlier, I gave examples of a New York restaurant manager helping the food-delivery worker unload boxes, a mail carrier ringing the doorbell to check in on an elderly individual living alone and an IKEA store using its display rooms as homes for stray dogs. HR departments often disallow or at least frown upon these practices. Properly leading job purposing, then, sometimes involves defying internal protocols and policies. As Will, put it, "The purpose-driven leader has to be willing to become an HR nightmare."

The purpose-driven leader has to be willing to be an HR nightmare.

-Will Hockney

Neither Noprag nor HP perform well on this Driver and this likely undermines the positive impact of their job purposing. It's not just the experiences of Charles and Will that suggest lack of tender leadership undermines leadership success. Evidence from hundreds of workers uncovered that tender leadership drives higher performance in workplaces spanning from the Taiwanese military to the U.S. technology sector.[129] It appears that a box of tissues is a new management tool.

Embrace Partial Alignment

WE GIVE IT represents the top job-purposing elements that drive employee engagement, performance, retention and other outcomes that managers value:

- **W**ork-related
- **E**mployee-crafted
- **G**roup-based
- **I**mpact-evident
- **V**iscerally-meaningful
- **E**volving
- **I**ntrospective
- **T**enderly-led

An indication of the importance of these Drivers is the fate of HP's and Noprag's job-purposing programs. HP's Eco Advocates is still thriving in its twelfth year. In fact, HP expanded the program from Canada to all countries and from the sales team to all departments. Tellingly, HP also renamed the program Sustainability Sells. Noprag's job purposing, on the other hand, lasted only five years. Without a good business justification for keeping the program, Noprag's leadership eventually retired it. Job purposing that aligns with the Drivers is likely an enduring business success. Job purposing that doesn't align with the Drivers will improve the state of the world and the personal lives of employees, but is unlikely to strengthen the business.

Don't fret, however, if your job purposing doesn't meet all eight Drivers. As you know, Eco Advocates isn't tenderly-led (Driver 8) and performs only moderately well on several other Drivers. Yet, it's a smashing success. Furthermore, as covered earlier, Caesars Entertainment has data showing that Luz and other housekeepers who participate in the program that collects soap for sterilization, repackaging and distribution to low-income families have higher employee engagement than those who don't. Yet, this program performs well only on WGIV (work-related, group-based, impact-evident and viscerally-meaningful). Similarly, work that I did with three companies in Europe and Latin America found that job purposing that met only WGET (work-related, group-based, evolving and tenderly-led) boosted employee engagement by 20 percent. Simply put, meeting half the Drivers at even a basic level appears to achieve meaningful workplace results. That said, the third Driver (group-based) is the most important single Driver and the first four are the most important half. So, if all of WE GIVE IT isn't feasible, G (group-based) should be the top priority and WEI (work-related, employee-crafted and impact-evident) the next priority.

Also, per the research presented in chapter three, we should keep in mind that job purposing that meets none of the Drivers will likely contribute to the personal lives of our team members. It will still boost their happiness and health even if it doesn't increase their direct value to the business. From the world's perspective, if not the employer's, even job purposing that meets none of the Drivers is worthwhile.

There is one final part to the day the boy high fived the wall I was painting with the Caesars team.

Beyond Success and Wellness

On the drive home from the Caesars Las Vegas volunteer project, Doug and I scan the road for a nice restaurant to celebrate my birthday. We don't find one. Instead, we sit in a vinyl-lined booth and eat pancakes drenched in artificial syrup, hop back in the car and drive in such slow-moving traffic that it doubles the trip to Southern California from three to six hours. At midnight, we are still several hours from home.

Shockingly, the entire evening is blissful. I feel like nothing can ruin my giddiness. All strangers are charming and every small blessing—whether a warm meal served by an awkward teenager, a peppy song on the sound system, a comfortable passenger seat or a late-night latte—is a sensuous luxury. While Doug drives us home, I draft a new speech that ends up becoming a bestseller. I know to expect a boost in wellness and performance from acts of social purpose. But this feels like a more profound shift—it's as though I've fundamentally become a more complete and content version of myself. It's as if something inside me has clicked into place. Over the next week, I become the moderately discontented self that I typically am. But probably less so than before volunteering at the school.

It turns out that job purposing doesn't just improve our daily lives. Over time, job purposing restores a vital part of our being so neglected we didn't even notice its absence.

IV. EVOLVING: THE ULTIMATE REASON TO JOB PURPOSE

Chapter 12

BECOMING OUR TRUE SELVES

*T*he poet David Whyte says, "The consummation of work lies not only in what we have done, but who we have become while accomplishing the task."[130] As covered in the first three sections of this book, it's well established that job purposing helps us accomplish more and become healthier and happier. But job purposing's most profound contribution is that it helps us become the whole beings we are meant to be.

The Inner Giver

I'm nine years old and staring out the window of my family's air-conditioned sedan trying to tune out my chattering twin sisters with whom I share the backseat. Sipping syrupy soda through a blue-and-

149

The consummation of work lies not only in what we have done, but who we have become while accomplishing the task.

-David Whyte

white-striped straw, I have no idea my superficially cheerful childhood is about to end.

A boy enters the frame of my window as our car inches along the Caracas highway, a still figure between rigid rows of cars crawling past him. He is about my size but with tattered shorts, no shirt and no shoes. A cardboard tray holding bags of potato chips hangs from his neck to rest just above his dirty belly, which is strangely large for his spindly body. His left elbow is bruised and swollen and makes me wince. His big brown eyes lock onto mine, softly questioning.

My thoughts wail like an emergency siren. Why is a kid my age selling chips on a dangerous highway? Why is he caked in dirt? Where are his Nike shoes? Why isn't his mother cleaning, bandaging and planting a get-well kiss on his injury? Why isn't he safely inside a car drinking something sweet through a striped straw? It's the first time I feel the tightness in my sternum that I've felt when distressed since then.

Our eyes track each other until he slips beyond my window. I regret not opening the car door and sharing my drink, shoes and world of comfort with the boy. I name him Raul and softly cry the rest of the way home.

What exactly happened to me during that encounter with an underprivileged peer? Seventeenth-century English philosopher Thomas Hobbes would have said that my parents, teachers and the rest of society civilized me into caring.[131] He would say that I was born purely selfish and it took society nine years to reform me into a caring individual. I mention this because the U.S. Constitution, almost all modern governments, the core of capitalism and most educational systems embody Hobbes' dismal view of human nature. Most of us had no choice but to internalize a Hobbesian mindset as unwittingly and unknowingly as we do a regional accent or convention of using certain eating utensils. We believe, think it's self-evident even, that humans are naturally selfish and conflictual. We think we need society to mold us into more civilized behavior. To determine if our Hobbesian outlook is right, I would like to share a story about Peony—or, rather, Peony's friends.

Because Peony is elderly and moves with difficulty, her buddies get her what she needs and steady her hobble so she can attend social gatherings and otherwise get around. Again, Hobbes would have said that these individuals are caring and helpful thanks to the civilizing influences of society. However, he was wrong. These helpers have never heard a parent, teacher or minister preach the virtues of kindness. Peony and company are chimpanzees who live in Emory University's Yerkes Primate Center in Georgia.

It turns out that chimpanzees often serve others. The primatologist who shared Peony's story, Frans de Waal, has also documented that chimpanzees frequently choose collective rewards over purely self-serving ones.[132] Other researchers have found that chimpanzees will forgo some of their own food to feed a friend.[133] The Max Planck Institute for Evolutionary Anthropology in Germany found that most semi-wild chimpanzees would climb an eight-foot rope to help an unfamiliar human who was struggling to reach a stick.[134]

It's not just chimpanzees who instinctively care for others. Rhesus monkeys won't pull a chain that provides food if it also gives an electric shock to a companion. One monkey gave up food for twelve days to prevent harm to another.[135] Mammals are born with an innate response to care for others. The aforementioned Max Planck Institute study found that well before socialization takes hold, human toddlers act as the chimps do: They help the unfamiliar human retrieve the stick.

Despite what Hobbes believed, and many still do, my Raul incident wasn't the result of society stomping down my natural inclinations and overlaying them with better ones. Instead, the Raul incident awakened an "inner giver" that I had all along. It's the part of me that hears the world's needs and yearns to help. As extraordinary as my inner giver feels to me, it isn't. Even the most carefree among us can't avoid grieving over the sad lot of our world, empathizing with strangers in distress and feeling pulled to help right injustice and assuage suffering. Every human has an inner giver. Well, almost.

Between 1 and 3 percent of the population lack an inner giver. They're called sociopaths (or in official terminology, individuals with "antisocial personality disorder"). An inner-giver deficiency is precisely the medical definition of a sociopath: "Individuals who habitually and pervasively disregard or violate the rights and considerations of others without remorse."[136] Sociopaths, however, are the exception that proves that inner givers are the norm. We don't treat the absence of an inner giver lightly. We label it mental illness and consider it abnormal.

In other words, the inner giver is a cornerstone of human normality. We were born with an inner giver. As we'll see, it shapes our lives in profound ways.

Portrait of the Inner Giver

Why did I wince when I saw Raul's injured arm? The same area in the brain that decades later made my arm ache when I broke it snowboarding transmitted pain signals when I saw Raul's injury. My cells responded similarly to Raul's injured arm as they did to my own.

It turns out that our brains have specialized cells to ensure we feel for others. These "mirror neurons" exist to replicate the experience of others in our own bodies. Hobbes would be shocked to learn we're born with the ability to feel someone else's pain. Christian Keysers, head of the Social Brain Lab at the Netherlands Institute for Neuroscience, explains: "As Westerners in particular, we are brought up to center our thinking on individuals—individual rights, individual achievements. But if you call the state of your brain your identity (and I would), what our research shows is that much of it is actually what happens in the minds of other people."[137]

Our sympathetic hardwiring is so strong it trumps our brainpower and willpower. Try as we might to stay calm when watching the fictional thug threaten the fictional hero in a Martin Scorsese movie, most of us cannot. We know it's absurd to be concerned about a person who doesn't exist. Still, our hearts race, our muscles tense and our breathing catches as if we were the character in peril.

Mirror neurons, however, are merely the foundation of what I call our "inner giver," our natural tendency to care about and contribute toward the wellbeing of others. That our brains reward us when we pursue social purpose (with dopamine, serotonin and oxytocin, for example, as covered in chapter three) is another aspect of our inner giver. Cognitive empathy, or our ability to think about how it might feel to be in someone else's shoes, is yet another aspect of our inner giver. I confess that inner giver is not the scientific term for the collection of social-purpose tendencies we innately have. I couldn't get myself to use the clumsy academic terms of "homo empathicus," "prosocial inclination" or "cognitive, affective and compassionate empathy." Also, my choice of inner giver is an homage to an icon in our understanding of social-purpose behavior, the Wharton organizational psychologist I've referenced several times, Adam Grant. He calls people who routinely contribute to others without expecting anything in return, "givers."

Our inner giver is formidable and concrete. It's not a spiritual belief, like a guardian angel. It's not an unproven theoretical concept, like the shortcut between two distant regions of space-time known as a wormhole. Specialized cells, blood components and brain matter make our inner givers as real as eyesight.

The Inner Giver vs the Inner Egotist

We might be innately endowed with an inner giver, but how significant a part of our psyche is it? Is the inner giver as vital to our psyche as lungs are to our physiology? As ancillary as earlobes are? Somewhere in between? After all, our psyches also have an "inner egotist." Our inner egotist is the part of us that is comfortable harming others for personal gain. It doesn't believe in wiping down the workplace microwave after splattering it with pizza sauce or in sharing credit with other team members. The same day Raul called forth my inner giver, I may have refused to share my drink with my sisters, pulled their hair or kicked them in the shins. The chimpanzees who cared for Peony are also known to bicker, fight and even kill each other. Which is dominant? Are we born primarily inner givers or inner egotists? This debate has rung through the ages. Fortunately, modern science has an answer.

Nature promotes our survival by ensuring that evolutionarily productive acts feel good. Eating and having sex are pleasurable to ensure that we don't starve to death or forget to reproduce. Between two actions, whichever one feels better is generally more fundamental to our existence. Using that measure, the inner giver easily beats our inner egotist. As covered in chapter three, the actions of our inner givers reduce the brain's stress response, flood us with feel-good hormones and generate joy. The actions of inner egotists, on the other hand, don't give us a natural high. On the contrary, hurting others is usually unpleasant and can generate shame, remorse and other negative feelings that persist long after the act (unless we are sociopaths).

The speed and ease with which we choose an action is another indication of how innate the action is. The inner giver wins this contest as well. A study conducted by the University of Michigan's Department of Psychology and Harvard's Center for Brain Science found that chimpanzees made cooperative decisions faster than selfish ones.[138] We are the same way. We don't wrestle with the decision of sending a thank-you card but might easily deliberate for hours or days before sending a potentially hurtful email.

Additional evidence that our inner giver plays a larger role than our inner egotist comes from examining our values. One researcher conducted a comprehensive study of what values people in eighty-two countries consider most important. Every country had essentially the same top value: enhancing the welfare of others.[139] That social purpose is our most important value regardless of culture—whether we go to a house of worship or not, discipline children in Urdu or Spanish, or eat fish or donuts for breakfast—suggests that it's not socialization that gives our inner givers top status. We do this innately.

In other words, there is strong evidence that the inner giver naturally has more authority over our lives than the inner egotist. It has for as long as we've been human, as covered next.

The Long Reign of the Inner Giver

Imagine our ancestors gathered around a campfire 20,000 years ago. An older woman plays with twin toddlers so their mother can relax for a moment. Young men distribute freshly picked berries. Two men happily tend the fire for all to enjoy. Inner givers run the show. Those of us questioning the validity of such a peaceful depiction of prehistoric life were most likely good students. He may have been disproven, but Hobbes' view of man as a selfish beast continues to dwell in textbooks.

We are taught that before civilization reached a certain level of moral sophistication, our lives were short, violent, painful and generally grim.

For example, could pre-agrarian humans really spend time lolling about a campfire? Weren't they busy trying to survive? Well, anthropologists have now uncovered that hunter-gatherers spent only between twenty and forty hours a week securing water, food, shelter, clothing and whatever else their survival required. What did they do for the remaining seventy-plus waking hours? They played games, talked, participated in religious ceremonies, made music, danced, visited friends in other tribes and took naps.[140] That is, they enjoyed being with each other.

What about the young men sharing berries? Why weren't they securing more food for themselves and their families by hacking each other with their stone axes? Again, it appears that there was rarely a need to take food from others in pre-agrarian societies. Food was typically plentiful for the few million humans spread across the planet. Prehistoric humans experienced hunger at times, but rarely the threat of starvation. As Boston College research psychologist Peter Gray put it, "The life of the typical hunter-gatherer looks a lot like your life and mine when we are on vacation at a camp with friends."[141] The status quo of prehistoric society was being noncompetitive, nonviolent and supportive of each other. It had more inner-giver than inner-egotist activity.

So, yes, the evidence suggests that my Norman Rockwell fireside scene really happened in prehistory. And quite often. Not only do we have inner givers, they have long been our default captains. Nevertheless, my peaceful campfire scene is not the full story of our prehistoric ancestors.

The Secondary and Vital Role of the Inner Egotist

A few hours into the fireside social gathering, someone notices that the man scheduled to guard against external threats, Zog, is not at his post. This is the third time this season that Zog has failed to show up for his job. Tribe members suddenly feel vulnerable to tigers and other threats lurking beyond the light of the fire. Scared and angry, their brains secrete cortisol and adrenaline to prepare for a fight. Women gather their young. Incensed over the unnecessary danger, a group of men sprint to Zog's cave, drag him to the edge of the wilderness, beat him bloody and expel him from the tribe. As an injured and solitary human in the wild, he's unlikely to live another year.

As covered earlier, if our inner egotist were our natural leader, the men who beat Zog would have enjoyed it or at least been unaffected by it. We know, however, that their violence was stressful and likely increased their chances of suffering from mental anguish, post-traumatic stress disorder (PTSD) and depression. How do we know this? By studying individuals having to similarly use force to restore order and having virtually identical genetics: modern police officers (human evolutionary changes do not occur within 20,000 years). Research finds that killing or injuring others, even when necessary for the public good, is a driver of PTSD and depression in police officers.[142]

I don't deny that some of us voluntarily injure and even kill others, sometimes with no apparent regret or remorse. We engage in police brutality, hate crime, domestic violence and other forms of deliberate harm. We don't only hurt others when necessary. We are also capable of inflicting gratuitous injury. This hardly means, however, that violence is our natural state or primary inclination. It merely means that there is a fragility to us. Any of us can stray from our default state, both temporarily and permanently. But instances of excessive violence aren't proof that we aren't primarily inner giver any more than instances of crawling are proof that we aren't primarily upright walkers.

Anthropological and psychological evidence increasingly suggests that nature has given our inner egotist the secondary role of security guard.[143] Our inner egotist is designed to be on the sidelines brandishing its brawn while our inner giver does things like hold the elevator for a colleague. But if the colleague is our cutthroat competitor for a promotion, our inner egotist might step in to shut the elevator door on them. We might briefly enjoy this rudeness. Still, there is little doubt (per chapter three) that we are generally happier and healthier when we are helping, as opposed to hurting, others.

Our inner givers and inner egotists are the complementary forces that ensured human survival over hundreds of thousands of years. We needed to care for one another and we needed to disable threats among us. We still do. Both our inner givers and egotists have mighty roles, but the default captain has long been our inner giver. As Robert Sussman, professor of anthropology at Washington University, puts it, "Human groups are much more likely to live in peace than in war."[144] Why, then, does it seem like the world is run amok by inner egotists?

Inner Givers Call the Shots

A steady stream of unconscionable acts, from Wall Street embezzlement to double murders, dominates our news feed day after day. It might feel like unbridled inner egoists rule the planet, but they don't.

By definition, what's newsworthy is unusual. Imagine seeing a news segment about a stocky man, Larry, walking out his front door into soft rain, rolling his empty trash bin from the curb to the back of the driveway and doing the same for his neighbor. All the while, he is on the phone saying, "Of course I'll loan you my mower. Come pick it up anytime." After he hangs up, he notices that the teenage boys who live down the street don't have umbrellas for their walk to their high school. Larry waves them over and insists on giving them a ride. It sounds boring. Many of us have witnessed something similar to this scene from our kitchen windows. But it was so mundane that it didn't make us look up from our electronic device for more than an instant, interrupt our meal or leave much of an impression on our busy brains. No one would consider creating a news story out of Larry's early morning.

A video of pillaging, injuring and killing, on the other hand, might be riveting and keep us glued to the screen. Why? Because these acts are exceptions to ordinary life. It's likely we've heard of Bernie Madoff swindling thousands of investors out of their life savings but not of Sarah Hemminger helping thousands of underprivileged youth succeed beyond their wildest dreams. The antics of inner egotists are newsworthy and those of inner givers are not.

It's not just the media that favors the negative. We all do. Consider our drive to work. One jerk cutting us off inspires the "can-you-believe?" story we tell coworkers. The eighty drivers who could have cut us off and chose not to, on the other hand, do not prompt us to tell a laudatory story. The excessive attention we give hurtful behavior is like wearing grey-colored glasses. It makes us believe we are among nasty, brutish people even when we're not. And the vast majority of us during the vast majority of time, are not. Contrary to the world view that Hobbes talked us into, we are most often surrounded by caring and cooperative people.

Our tilt toward the negative is not a conscious decision. We're hypersensitive to threats because, in terms of evolution, it's more critical to avoid death than to relish the benign. For starters, we're imbued with what psychologists call "negativity bias." That is, we give greater weight to negative than to positive acts. For example, we notice pain but rarely notice an absence of pain. As if negativity bias didn't darken our outlook enough, we also have what Stanford University psychologist Amos Tversky and Daniel Kahneman, the Nobel laureate mentioned in chapter two, termed "availability heuristic." This cognitive snag confuses the strength of a memory with the frequency of its occurrence. As a result, we think anything shocking, like violence and betrayal, is more commonplace than it is. In other words, the stories we circulate disproportionally draw from the antics of our inner egotists. In reality, inner givers call most of the shots most of the time in most places.

A company that sells iced tea and other beverages, Honest Tea, put up shelves stocked with their drinks in twenty-four U.S. cities. These stations were unmanned but had signage specifying that the drinks cost one dollar and a bin to insert payment. Per the proportion of buyers who voluntarily paid for their drinks, every city was over 82 percent honest and the national average was 93 percent honest.[145] Admittedly, Honest Tea's marketing ploy can hardly be considered rigorous research. Academic studies, however, yield similar results. In one study, researchers deliberately lost 17,000 wallets containing ninety-four dollars in local currency across 40 countries. Seventy-two percent of those who found the wallets returned them with the money they contained.[146] In other words, even in circumstances where there are no obvious negative consequences, selfish behavior is the exception.

We might think that people would be more likely to keep the wallets if they contained more money, but the above 40-country study found the exact opposite is true. As outlandish as it might sound to our cynical minds, this finding suggests that we are more interested in minimizing a stranger's loss than in maximizing our personal gain. We know that a fourteen-dollar loss won't be terribly damaging to the owner. But because losing ninety-four dollars might cause hardship, we try harder to get it back to the unknown owner. That's how dominant our inner giver is over our inner egotist. Most of the time, most of us would return a lost wallet, even if no one was watching. Our innate inner givers are typically more active than our inner egotists. This is our natural and happiest state.

Our Inner Givers Are Largely Absent at Work

Unfortunately, our inner givers are somewhat dormant and our inner egotists are mostly dominant at our workplaces—a mainstage of our lives. At work, we often don't feel comfortable doing the equivalent of returning the wallet. This undermines our performance, health and happiness per the research presented in chapter three. It also, unfortunately, prevents us from being fully ourselves and feeling complete.

Larry, the hypothetical good neighbor, might be unrecognizable at work. Two glass soda bottles lay next to where he parks. He doesn't pick them up. On his way to his cubicle, he walks by a dozen employees from another department (procurement, he suspects), as he has every day for months. He doesn't greet any of them. When he visits the restroom midmorning, a janitor five feet away struggles to open a cardboard box of paper towels. Larry says, "good morning," but doesn't think to hold the box for him. He and another sales representative are early for a meeting, but Larry doesn't ask how the colleague is holding up through a divorce. None of these actions, which come naturally in other settings, even occur to the Larry that inhabits the workplace. He doesn't do the workplace equivalent of returning the lost wallet. Workplace Larry doesn't have the benefit of his inner giver.

Larry is not an insensitive jerk. He's merely responding to his environment. In many workplaces, picking up parking-lot litter, greeting strangers in cubicles, helping the janitor or asking a colleague about her personal life would be considered aberrant. Workplaces are unwelcoming to inner givers. Specifically, they exclude our inner giver in three main ways:

1. **Structured Out**

    Most of our ancestors benefitted from work perfectly structured for their inner givers. Prehistoric Hal ran abreast with others through the forest to secure food for a public feast, started bonfires with his buddies for all their families to enjoy and helped neighbors repair the roof of another neighbor.

Hal's work was done collectively for the common good. It inherently had social purpose woven through it. On the other hand, modern-day Larry spends his workday holding sales meetings in pursuit of his individual bonuses, promotions and dreams. In other words, many modern work roles aren't a good fit for inner givers (unless they are job purposed).

2. **Crowded Out**

A group of students is asked to go to another building to deliver a speech. On their way, an actor sits slumped in a doorway, head down, eyes closed and not moving. As the students walk by, the actor coughs and groans. This Princeton University experiment found that students who possessed one specific thing were six times more likely to help than those who didn't. Was this thing religious faith? Extroversion? Stronger ethics? Two X chromosomes? A vegetarian diet?

None of the above. The helpers had time. Students who had ample time to get to the appointment were six times more likely to stop (63 percent did) than those who were pressed for time (10 percent).[147] In other words, haste stifles our inner giver.

As mentioned earlier, prehistoric Hal's schedule was fairly loose. He had time to detect and act on the needs of others. Unfortunately, Larry and the rest of us modern workers usually have such compressed work schedules that our inner givers can't find an opening through which to emerge. All the while we miss opportunities to contribute to others and fully become ourselves.

3. **Shunned**

The grey-bearded foreman in the front row sprints to the podium as soon as I conclude my presentation. "You were a perfect ten," he tells me. "Until fifteen minutes ago. Then you blew it." He holds his session evaluation up to my face. Under the "overall assessment" one-to-ten scale, the ten is obscured under a blot of black ink, and the four is circled.

What made my final few minutes so heinous that my performance plummeted 60 percent to mediocrity? Emotion. In the concluding exercise, participants planned ways to help a colleague who lost his home to fire. It was impossible not to be moved by the display of compassion. Some workers, including a few husky men, sniffled and wiped away tears.

"That exercise was unprofessional. This is a workplace. We can't afford to have weepy workers," the foreman roars at me. He then pivots and storms out of the room. The foreman wants a workplace with social purpose but insists on an emotionally sterile culture. This is akin to wanting to snuggle up to a Saint Bernard without getting slobbered on. If we want the warm fuzzies, we need to tolerate a little sloppiness.

Job purposing changes us precisely because it's *not* a tidy abstraction that leaves us unaffected. On the contrary, as covered in chapter three, helping a homeless colleague or pursuing some other social purpose is so moving that it alters blood chemistry. The same physiological response that makes us more motivated, healthy and happy also produces goosebumps, sniffles, awkward hugs and the weepiness the foreman dreads.

Unfortunately, many managers don't realize that a sense of social purpose cannot flourish in the emotional deserts they consider efficient workplaces. Instead of exercising the tender leadership that Charles and Will (from chapter eleven) do, many managers would consider it a weakness and a mistake to allow their voice to quiver when announcing layoffs or to otherwise show they care. Modern managers often impede job purposing by insisting on emotionally neutral workplaces, even when they have bought into the need for igniting social purpose in their workplace.

What's especially tragic about the workplace excluding our inner giver is that work is its natural habitat. Work is where our inner giver is designed to thrive. It might even be the only place it can, as covered next.

Work Devoid of Social Purpose Isn't Natural, Productive, Healthy or Human

Work has always been a platform for contributing to others. As covered earlier, prehistoric jobs made life easier and better for the tribe as a whole. Virtually all work was inherently job purposed. As a result, prehistoric work *felt* good. According to anthropologists, pre-agrarian work didn't feel distinctly different from playing with the kids or drawing on a cave wall. Indeed, it appears that work felt so much like leisure that hunter-gatherer languages didn't even have a word for it.[148] It is our evolutionary legacy to do good and feel good at work.

What's more, work might be the *only* place modern full-time workers can pursue social purpose. If we don't make meaningful contributions at work, it's unlikely we will make them at all. According to the U.S. Bureau of Labor Statistics, after accounting for work, professional development and commuting, U.S. full-time workers have about 111.2 available hours a week. Subtracting the time it takes us to do household chores (15.5 hours a week); eat (8.3 hours); shop for groceries and other necessities (5.3 hours); bathe and groom (5.2 hours), care for children and other family members (4.8 hours) and exercise (2.2 hours) leaves 69.9 hours.[149] Our remaining time after completing essential activities, then, is 10.0 hours per day. But we haven't slept a wink, posted anything on social media, seen any movies, read any books, caught up on the news, watched our favorite sports team or called a single friend. Unless those of us who work full-time are willing to give up our sleep, leisure or friends, work might be our only outlet for pursuing social purpose.

In other words, releasing our inner givers at work isn't unnatural or illogical. Work is where our inner givers evolved and where they belong.

Job Purposing Is the Inner Shift We Need

When my brother Alfredo was sixteen, he disassembled a derelict Volkswagen beetle with the intent of transforming it into a functioning vehicle. It didn't go as planned.

After months of tools clanking, the engine roars to life. Success! Well, sort of. The car runs, but with a quirk. It has four gears in reverse and one in drive. Alfredo inverted some part in the transmission. The entire family is amused, but no one more than the self-effacing Alfredo. With a twinkle in his eye and keys in his outstretched hand, he offers, "Want to drive fifty miles per hour in reverse?" I take the keys.

I back out of our driveway onto the streets of Caracas and do my best. Everything is a struggle. With the steering wheel doing the opposite of what I expect, I meander side to side. Having to turn my head 180 degrees is unpleasant. The massive blind spot is frightening. I don't know how fast I manage to go because the dash is behind my head, but I doubt it's more than fifteen miles per hour. After ten minutes, my neck aches, I'm exhausted and, judging from the honks, intensely disliked.

At work, most of us suffer from an inversion similar to that of Alfredo's beloved bug. Our inner egotist and inner giver roles are reversed. We rely on our inner egotists to drive our careers. Yet, the inner egotist is more like a reverse gear. It's designed for episodic maneuvering, mostly out of tight spots. It's not good at cruising forward and can't give us the wind-in-our hair, joyful ride of our lives. When we succeed by the power of our inner egotist, we're doing so the hard way. Our journey is unnecessarily shaky, unpleasant, frightening, slow and painful. Many of us mistakenly believe this is normal and inevitable.

I asked Charles Antis, the founder and CEO of Antis Roofing (discussed in chapter eleven), how work felt after his pivot toward social purpose compared to before. He said it felt like "a relief." The Chocolate Angel, the woman who goes to worksites to deliver small treats and her undivided attention to workers, also said her transition to social-purpose work was a relief. I believe it's our inner giver and inner egotist clicking into their rightful spots at the workplace that generates such a profound sense of relief.

Scaling Job Purposing

Imagine a laborer arriving for his first workday on the construction site of the Golden Gate Bridge in 1933. You ask him, "What do you think of construction workers having protective hardhats and a safety net to catch their falls?" His likely response would be, "What's a hardhat? What's a safety net?" In 1933 workplace safety was a fringe idea. But thanks to the vision of the chief engineer of the Golden Gate Bridge, that worker benefitted from those two safety features and his chances of dying on the job dropped by 69 percent.[150]

The chief engineer of the Golden Gate Bridge, Joseph Strauss, insisted on implementing new safety measures for his workers, including a net spanning the bridge's entire length of over a mile and a half. The safety net caught nineteen workers before they would have plummeted into the water with a 98 percent certainty of death. Strauss refused to accept that inherently dangerous jobs had to remain so. His compassionate action, combined with similar efforts from many others, helped force an evolution in worker safety that we continue to benefit from. That same bridge-building job is seventy times less likely to kill us today than it was a few generations back. Joseph Strauss' story shows that, historically speaking, radical workplace improvements happen.

Our current jobs are the result of a sequence of workplace transformations over hundreds of years. In its dawn, each emerging improvement appeared as dubious as standardizing job purposing might seem now. Yet, those transformations happened. And so can widespread job purposing. We are now aware of an unmet employee need: work that matters, that does good. Like Strauss, we can take action. We can make job purposing as much the status quo as workplace safety has become.

Chapter 13

CHANGING THE WORLD

*I*t's established: We all need social purpose, most of us aren't getting it and job purposing can meet this need. But job purposing is only secondarily about us. It's primarily about what Raul, the child who endured unimaginable hardship selling potato chips on a Caracas highway, represents. The weightiest reason to job purpose is to transform the underbelly of the human experience. It's to help those suffering from poverty, unemployment, disease, grief, depression, addiction, inequity, discrimination or other hardship. It's about restoring the natural state of our rivers, creating healthy communities and relishing each other. But can job purposing really do these things? It can.

If our job purposing lightens the load for just one person this month, that is impact enough. A short conversation with that lucky person will make that abundantly clear. Thanks to the pivot, ripple and drizzle effects, however, our job purposing will likely accomplish much more. No, these are not three things to do at a pool party. They are something better.

The Power of the Pivot

The bridge engineer Joseph Strauss didn't improve the world by doing something monumental. Introducing safety practices at one worksite was a small step, even if that site was building what would become the iconic Golden Gate Bridge. The power of Strauss' action was in its pivot. By taking a step in a new direction, he put us on a path to a future in which workplace safety is a human right.

When we job purpose, even modestly, we're similarly inviting people to turn toward a brighter direction, one they didn't necessarily know existed. Once reoriented toward social purpose, people will astonish us. They will add a twist, apply a new context or otherwise evolve what we started. Workers have outdone whatever job purposing I initiated at every company I've worked with. Where else would I have found the over 100 examples of job purposing presented in this book?

Strauss didn't put up smoke detectors, establish workplace air-quality standards or invent ergonomic keyboards. Yet, these widespread safety practices go back, in part, to the vision he put forth of a workplace that didn't kill or maim anyone. It's easy to underestimate small acts of job purposing. Yet, they permanently pivot history toward the positive. And this is just the beginning of the good our job purposing unleashes.

The Reach of the Ripple

William is an eighteen-year-old busboy. As happens in many workplaces in December, William's colleagues swap stories about holiday plans—who they will visit, what gifts they will give and what food they will eat. This happy talk puts William in an uncomfortable situation.

The patriarch of his family, William's grandfather, has recently died and his mother has moved away. Earning five dollars an hour, William is the breadwinner for himself, his grandmother and his ten-year-old brother. They can barely afford their pay-by-the-week motel room. The family has always celebrated Christmas, but this year they can't afford to.

What does William do when the servers, hostesses, supervisors and others ask about his holiday plans? Too embarrassed about the truth, he lies. The busboy prattles on about the guitar he will get, the new shoes he will give his brother and the traditional gelatin salad his grandmother will serve for dessert.

About a week before Christmas day, William arrives at work to find a stack of wrapped boxes. His colleagues bought and wrapped every item he lied about. Incredulous, William asks his coworkers why they did it. They respond, "Because you are one of us and so is your family." A decade later, William is the successful casino manager featured in chapter eleven whose job purposing has, at its core, the concept that colleagues are family. William is Will Hockney. He credits this Christmas story for his job-purposed management.

The coworkers who helped Will's family years ago created a ripple through time. They are responsible for a tightly knit marketing team at a casino in Cleveland that routinely brightens the lives of others. What's more, the acts the casino team performs now are sending ripples into the future. Our job purposing doesn't just improve the lives of those lucky enough to be there for it.

To measure the magnitude of the ripple effect, researchers enrolled over eighty workers at a plant in Madrid in a study. The workers were asked to write down their moods and any acts of generosity they performed each day. Researchers then arranged for a random half of participants to receive, on average, one extra act of kindness a week for a month. These acts were modest, such as being surprised with a mid-afternoon pastry or receiving help creating a purchase order.

After a few weeks, the lucky workers who received the extra dosage of good deeds performed almost three times more social-purpose acts than those in the comparison group who did not receive the extra dosage.[151] The triple contributors would, logically, create another group of triple contributors who would create yet another group of triple contributors and so on. In other words, our job purposing will do good well beyond what we know and probably can imagine. Thanks to the ripple or multiplier effect, job purposing helps a potentially infinite number of people.

We might think that some people won't even feel the ripple, much less allow themselves to be affected by it. They might be too set in their ways, too narrow in their estimation of possibilities and too jaded in their attitudes. There are people who will fail to respond to the pivot or the ripple. However, the drizzle might still move these stubborn laggards. I know because I was one of them.

The Persuasiveness of the Drizzle

I'm finally under the covers, as inert as an overcooked vegetable, in my hotel bed. My mind relaxes into the sleep I ache for. Ahhh.

Then I hear it. I'm startled awake. Irate. "Ugh. I last slept 3,000 air miles and twenty-two hours ago. I'm too tired for this." I decide to pretend I never heard the alarming noise. No one will know. The hotel won't charge for my neglect. My plan fails. The sound keeps jarring me awake. Not because it's loud, but because of what it means. I hear the scorching of the world.

Wanting fresh air, I opened the window earlier but forgot to turn off the thermostat. What my mind considers an alarm is nothing more than the soft hum of the heating system. I can't fall asleep to the image of a refinery spewing gunk into the air to generate the warmth I'm wasting. I'm disturbed that I'm pumping seventy-degree air into the fifty-degree Dallas night. I'm upset that I'm warming the globe.

I will my weary limbs out of the warm bed, scamper across the cold floor to the thermostat and move the dial toward a better world. It's not a heroic act, but it's more than I would have done ten years ago. The younger Bea would have thought, "I won't get charged for my wastefulness" and allowed the heat's hum to lull her to sleep.

What changed? Why can I no longer be the insensitive energy consumer I once was? It wasn't my choice. As a young adult, I had no interest in the vulnerabilities of nature. The college Earth Day organizers in faded tee shirts struck me as freaky bores. I looked askance at the tables they set up in the cafeteria with signs like "Compost your waste" and said to my friends, "Eeewww. That's so gross." Clearly, I did not see the need for environmental sustainability.

Albert Einstein had an explanation for the dynamic between early environmentalists and me: "Great spirits always encounter violent opposition from mediocre minds."[152] Those early environmentalists were the great spirits. They were aware of a little-known truth and courageous enough to stand up for it. I was the mediocre mind, incapable of appreciating a worthy nudge.

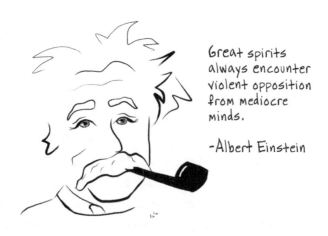

Great spirits always encounter violent opposition from mediocre minds.

-Albert Einstein

Yet, eventually, I got it. In the way a steady drizzle softens a hardened field, environmentalists changed me. Each of their articles in airline magazines, posters on trailheads, explanations over dinner tables and hundreds of other messages, dissolved my stubbornness a smidgen more. In addition to shutting off the thermostat when my windows are open, I now recycle, don't set the heat any higher than seventy degrees, avoid consuming single-use plastic and practice other acts of environmental protection.

Whatever societal injustice we address with our job purposing, whether it's the treatment of animals, racial prejudice or the global migration crisis, we shouldn't give up on others. At first, and for what might seem interminably long, some will smirk, argue and test our patience. Yet, meaningful causes eventually compel. Beneath the obsession with posting selfies, mindless consumerism and other superficiality dwells an inner giver designed to latch onto our job-purposing ideas. We shouldn't stop inviting, nudging and hoping. One day, many of the laggards will realize that climate change has our planet ablaze, and they'll bike to work. They'll understand the injustice of racism and organize unconscious-bias training. They'll hear our alarm, wake up and move the dial toward a better world.

Our Collective Efforts Will Change the World

But can all of this pivoting, rippling and drizzling add up to substantive improvements in the sorry state of the planet? After all, there's nothing new about people trying to right the ship of humanity. Religious, charitable and government organizations have been at it for centuries. What could the addition of job purposing do? Isn't it doing more of what hasn't worked, only now during business hours? I frequently get skeptical questions like these.

Only 6 percent of those in the United States and 10 percent of those on planet Earth believe we are improving the state of the world.[153]

Harvard cognitive psychologist Stephen Pinker says we suffer from "progressphobia." He's labeled our widespread pessimism a phobia because it's irrational. It's a knee-jerk rejection of the idea that our efforts can improve the lot of humanity. It's not based on facts.

The world *is* getting better. When I met Raul, the impoverished boy selling potato chips in the 1970s, his life expectancy would have him dead by now, in his fifties. But since that day, we have increased his life expectancy by four months every year, on average.[154] The net effect is that he's likely to be alive today and free of the poverty that marred his childhood. Life expectancy is just one instance of our progress. We are making similar strides across virtually every societal issue.

In September of 2000, the world set eight Millennium Development Goals to achieve by 2015: eradicate extreme poverty and hunger; achieve universal primary education; promote gender equality and empower women; reduce child mortality; improve maternal health; combat HIV/AIDS, malaria and other diseases; ensure environmental sustainability; and develop a global partnership for development. We haven't fully achieved these goals, but we've made substantive progress on all eight.[155] For example, in the fifteen years between 2000 and 2015 we:

- Halved the number of people living in extreme poverty.
- Lowered child mortality by 41 percent.
- Closed the gender gap in education in the developing world almost entirely.
- Reduced HIV infections by 35 percent.
- Lowered the malaria mortality rate by 58 percent.
- Reduced our use of ozone-depleting substances so dramatically that the ozone layer is on a trajectory to full recovery within two generations.

The world's millions of nonprofit and government organizations *are* fixing the world. Funding medical research, opening after-school programs, advocating for victims, teaching workplace skills, proposing legal protections for vulnerable populations and making endless appeals for donations add up to a lot of good. Increasing the dosage of these efforts by half might make this planet unrecognizably wonderful. Job purposing could conceivably accomplish this.

The private sector is a massive resource that is mostly untapped when it comes to directly promoting social purpose. For example, while the for-profit sector makes up over 60 percent of the U.S. economy (measured using Gross Domestic Product), its contributions add up to only 5 percent of nonprofit funding and 6 percent of federal tax revenue.[156] Similarly, the U.S. for-profit sector employs almost 80 percent of U.S. workers, four times the number of workers in the government and nonprofit sectors combined. This means that to increase the number of hours we collectively dedicate to societal issues by half, every for-profit worker would need to apply job purposing five hours a week. If this appears a daunting amount, it's because we are new to job purposing. Those experienced with job purposing typically discover that growing the practice to sixty minutes of activity per workday is feasible at most jobs. Many examples presented earlier—including Dawn the FedEx python patroller, Luz the Caesars housekeeper, most HP Eco Advocates and virtually every worker at Interface (the flooring company that committed to helping to reverse climate change)—exceed this threshold.

Were we to generalize five hours of job purposing a week across the private sector, the resulting 50 percent increase in the world's level of social-purpose effort would likely free the planet of extreme poverty, child mortality and malaria deaths within fifteen years. My calculation is simplistic and based on the data from one country. Still, my quantitative illustration makes a valid and globally applicable point: The business sector is so massive that if it conducts a modest amount of job purposing, it can dramatically expand the amount of social-purpose activity and lead to unimagined levels of human flourishing.

My belief that increasing our social-purpose efforts can be so consequential might sound naïve. But two experts that no one would accuse of naïveté—Steven Pinker, mentioned above, and Bill Gates, the co-founder of Microsoft and the Bill & Melinda Gates Foundation— have reached similar conclusions. Pinker combed through data on environmental degradation, illness, inequality, hunger, suffering, terrorism, tyranny, violence, war and more. His analysis found that over the last three hundred years (longer in most cases) our efforts have dramatically improved every issue.[157] Bill Gates, on the other hand, co-founded the largest social-purpose organization in the world, the Bill & Melinda Gates Foundation. His evidence-based reading of existing efforts to assuage societal issues, including in the most impoverished and war-torn places on the planet, has led him to conclude that our collective social-purpose efforts meaningfully move the needle in a positive direction.[158]

We may have a decade or two where crime, prejudice or other indicators of human wellness decline. We might find ourselves in a frightening pandemic or religious conflict from which human thriving appears improbable. Furthermore, most generations grapple with an issue that threatens to extinguish humanity altogether, such as a nuclear conflict or an unabated climate crisis. Our history, however, is consistent. Time and time again, we've tamed the dire threats, emerged from our grim setbacks and continued our upward trajectory. The facts are indisputable. On the whole, our social-purpose efforts make life better. Further endeavors, in all likelihood, will continue to do so.

Of course, every instance of job purposing might not improve the world. Some of my efforts have fallen flat. This is probably also true for

Papi, Oprah, the Chocolate Angel, Gwen and every other worker who has regularly job purposed. Yet, choosing to routinely job purpose allows us to look back at our years of labor secure that they lightened suffering at least a smidgen. Please trust the evidence: Our ongoing job purposing will improve the world.

Chapter 19

BECOMING WEIGHTLESS

Before the scorching Caracas sun shows its first rays through the hospital window, I sit on the daybed typing into my laptop. Papi stirs awake and asks, "What work are you doing in such darkness?" Unwilling to be called an imbecile, I don't share the idea I've been developing for about a year. "Nothing much," I say. He sighs.

In the white hospital bed, ensnarled in wires and flanked by beeping machines, Papi looks small and trapped. A pang of sympathy for the sick man I just snubbed lodges in my sternum. I will myself to be brave. Whatever insult he hurls at me, my sister will help me shrug it off within hours. Also, Papi is still the genius he's always been and the source of my idea. He might have good suggestions.

More poignantly, this might be the last time I talk to him. He's in a morbid limbo: scheduled to go into life-saving surgery for an aortic aneurism in a few hours, yet at risk of dying on the table from complications caused by his tobacco-damaged lungs. My inner giver urges me to give the man what he requested.

Papi interrupts my thoughts, "If you don't talk to me, I'll have to entertain myself." To my horror, he starts singing his old standard, "*Tengo una vaca lechera, no es una vaca cualquiera*," [I have a dairy cow, it's not just any cow]. It's mockingly soulful, raspy, off-key and dissonant. It's possibly the least calming lullaby ever sung. I'm half amused and half mortified.

"Papi, stop before you wake up every ailing soul in the ward!" I plead. "I'll tell you what I'm working on," I promise. The cacophony stops. It's too dark to see his expression, but I swear I hear his triumphant smile.

I start my soliloquy. "You taught me that anyone can do good from any job…" It's years before I give it a name or test its viability, but I'm babbling about an early version of job purposing. Despite what I told myself earlier, I care what Papi thinks. I care what everybody thinks. I hadn't yet collected the data on the transformative power of social purpose, but I had felt it. My work on social-purpose initiatives with a collection of companies gave me a tantalizing vision for how momentous purpose-infused labor might be. I can't look away from the bright light it seems to cast on the future of work. As I blather, I become aware that I desperately want to bring the joy of meaningful work to the stooped souls dutifully doing their chores across store counters, behind computer monitors, in toll booths and in every other crevice of our modern world.

"I think any worker in any job could go home secure that their day of labor mattered, that they matter," I state. I explain that through my work with Aetna, FedEx, HP, Levi's, Toyota and several other brands, I'm confident that this vision is feasible. Yet, an unanswered question has had me paralyzed for months. Helping workers do good from work is viable, but is it the right thing to do? I'm concerned it's unkind or even reckless. Workers have sore backs, needy children, leaky roofs and myriad other concerns. I fear that further burdening the already-burdened workers of the world with humanity's heart-wrenching problems will break them.

"Papi, are the world's problems too heavy a burden to place on the already stressed workers of the world? They have their own difficulties. I don't want to make things worse for them."

The room goes silent except for the mechanical beeps of medical equipment. I continue, "Think of Marcos." (The handyman who told me about my father standing up for him when he spilled a pail of water and setting up the inclusive game room.) "He struggled to feed his own family…" The morning sun has now bathed the room in a warm low light. I see that my dad shut his eyes. Convinced that I have been talking into a void, I stop.

But my father isn't sleeping. "You got it wrong," he says and clears his throat. I brace myself for the sharp "imbecile" jibe to launch from his lips and impale in my sternum. He continues, "*Mi cielito lindo*, Marcos found ways to contribute every day. That's what gave him the ability to rise above his circumstances."

Suddenly, I realize that Marcos job purposed. I think back to how, despite my shyness, Marcos got me to talk, lightened my mood and made me a proud daughter. I think of his chapped hands offering a manual pulled from his cardboard box. I, a privileged but painfully bashful child, benefitted from his kindness. His box was a stash of gifts for people encountered through work. Marcos was systemically job purposing. He was routinely pursuing social purpose and benefitting from the associated boost in success and wellbeing.

Papi coughs a few times before he sums up in a surprisingly strong voice. "Alleviating the burdens of the world doesn't burden us. It elates us."

Alleviating the burdens of the world doesn't burden us. It elates us.

-Papi

Until that moment, I didn't quite understand the advice my father had given me half a lifetime earlier. I had thought that "listen beyond the clamor of your wants for the whisper of the world's needs" was a reprimand to grow up and stop chasing frivolous fun, such as horseback riding. It turns out that Papi wasn't pointing me toward high morality, at least not exclusively, but toward the ultimate gallop.

I'm living proof of Papi's hospital lesson. I tried to transcend my bundle of burdens by riding horses, diving underwater and snowboarding mountainsides. These activities didn't produce the sensation of weightlessness I was chasing, but others did. A villager in the Philippines pointing at the saplings we just planted and telling her five-year-old daughter, "The shade and animals will return." A child in Nevada radiating pride because he goes to a school that is suddenly beautiful. A nonprofit director in New York thanking me for inspiring her banquet attendees to become even more committed to ending prejudice. These experiences freed me from myself. The burdened me always reappeared on the backside of those majestic moments, but a little lighter. It's as though every act of social purpose permanently raised every subsequent life experience ever so slightly.

I walked out of that hospital and into the sunlight with the answer to my dilemma. No matter the hardship workers face, the opportunity to do good at work—to untether from the lure of money, to positively imprint the world, to work buoyed by their inner giver, to leave a lyrical legacy and to transcend themselves at least fleetingly—is life-enriching. With the help of countless clients and colleagues, I researched, defined, tested and refined the concept of job purposing for over a decade to try to ensure it was worthy of consideration by the workers of the world. I confess that I didn't give up sliding down snowy slopes and otherwise pursuing pointless fun. But I did learn not to expect fulfillment from such hedonic activities. The irony is that they now delight me more than ever.

My father also walked out of that hospital and lived long enough to hear me report back, "Papi, job purposing works. In fact, I was asked to write a book about it!"

ABOUT THE AUTHOR

Bea Boccalandro advises business leaders on igniting social purpose in the workplace and helps workers end their workday knowing they made a difference. She has twenty years of experience helping to make customer interactions more human, products more inclusive, meetings more meaningful, operations more environmentally sustainable, marketing more charitable and otherwise tilting everyday work toward a meaningful contribution. This do-good-at-work practice, termed "job purposing," is a proven way to heighten workplace productivity, performance, satisfaction and personal wellbeing. It also improves business performance. Bea's clients include Aetna, Allstate, Bank of America, Caesars Entertainment, Disney, Eventbrite, FedEx, HP, John Hancock, IBM, Levi's, PwC and Toyota. Bea is founder and president of VeraWorks, a global firm

that helps businesses implement and measure the impact of pursuing social purpose. She is also a frequent keynote speaker and teaches at Georgetown University and the University of Nevada, Las Vegas. Bea can be seen drawing cartoons of innocent people anywhere she finds herself or trying to surf the waves of San Clemente, California, where she lives with her husband.

Learn more about Bea at www.BeaBoccalandro.com.

ENDNOTES

1   Unless explicitly cited as a fictional character, the individuals mentioned by name are actual people and their actions are factual, as best my memory, notes and fact-checking with those individuals and others served me. Full names are included for individuals that readers might want to learn more about (e.g., researchers and corporate leaders who excel in doing good at work). Otherwise, last names are omitted. Several first names were changed to pseudonyms for privacy or other reasons. I refer to people by their first name if I have a personal relationship with them. Otherwise, I use their last names.

2   The customary spelling of wellbeing in the United States is well-being. This book uses the nonhyphenated form of this word that is more common in the United Kingdom and other countries.

3   Happiness Research Institute and Krifa, "Job Satisfaction Index 2017," Happiness Research Institute, 2017.

4 Jonathan Rothwell and Steve Crabtree, "Not Just a Job: New Evidence on the Quality of Work in the United States," Lumina Foundation, the Bill & Melinda Gates Foundation, Omidyar Network, and Gallup, 2019.

5 Aaron Hurst and Nicole Resch, "2019 Workforce Purpose Index: Pathways to Fulfillment at Work," Imperative, 2019.

6 Archie Green, *Wobblies, Pile Butts, and Other Heroes: Laborlore Explorations* (Urbana: University of Illinois Press, 1993).

7 Karsten I. Paul and Klaus Moser, "Unemployment Impairs Mental Health: Meta-Analyses," *Journal of Vocational Behavior 74*, no. 3 (June 2009); Tony A. Blakely, Sunny C. D. Collings and June Atkinson, "Unemployment and Suicide. Evidence for a Causal Association?," *Journal of Epidemiology & Community Health 57*, no. 8 (July 2003); Lídia Farré, Francesco Fasani and Hannes Mueller, "Feeling Useless: The Effect of Unemployment on Mental Health in the Great Recession," *IZA Journal of Labor Economics 7*, no. 8 (2018); Olivera Batic-Mujanovic, Samir Poric, Nurka Pranjic, Enisa Ramic, Esad Alibasic and Enisa Karic, "Influence of Unemployment on Mental Health of the Working Age Population," *Materia Socio Medica* 29, no.2 (June 2017).

8 Studs Terkel, *Working: People Talk About What They Do All Day and How They Feel About What They Do* (New York: The New Press, 1997).

9 Alex Bryson and George MacKerron, "Are You Happy While You Work?" *The Economic Journal* 127, no. 599 (February 2017).

10 Gallup, "Work and Workplace, 2019," Gallup website, accessed on April 5, 2020.

11 Gartner, "Gartner Says Only 13% of Employees Are Largely Satisfied With Their Work Experiences," Gartner website, October 29, 2019, accessed on April 5, 2020.

12   Suzanne Mancini, "Do You Recommend Your Job to Others?" Effectory website, June 7, 2019, accessed on April 5, 2020.

13   Patrick van Kessel, Adam Hughes, Gregory A. Smith and Becka A. Alper, "Where Americans Find Meaning in Life," Pew Research Center, November 20, 2018.

14   Duncan S. Gilchrist, Michael Luca, and Deepak Malhotra, "When 3+1>4: Gift Structure and Reciprocity in the Field," *Management Science* 62, no. 9 (September 2016).

15   Timothy A. Judge, et al., "The Relationship Between Pay and Job Satisfaction: A Meta-Analysis of the Literature," *Journal of Vocational Behavior* 77 (2010).

16   Niklas Lollo and Dara O'Rourke, "Productivity, Profits, and Pay: A Field Experiment Analyzing the Impacts of Compensation Systems in an Apparel Factory," IRLE Working Paper no. 104-18, 2018.

17   WorldatWork, "WorldatWork 2018-2019 Salary Budget Survey," WorldatWork, 2018.

18   David A. Comerford and Peter A. Ubel, "Effort Aversion: Job Choice and Compensation Decisions Overweight Effort," *Journal of Economic Behavior & Organization* (August 2013).

19   Daniel Kahneman and Angus Deaton, "High Income Improves Evaluation of Life But Not Emotional Well-Being," *Proceedings of the National Academy of Sciences* 107, no. 38 (September 21, 2010).

20   Lindsay McGregor and Neel Doshi, *Primed to Perform: How to Build the Highest Performing Cultures Through the Science of Total Motivation* (New York: Harper Business, 2015); Gregory M. Walton, Geoffrey Cohen, David Cwir, and Steven Spencer, "Mere Belonging: The Power of Social Connections," *Journal of Personality and Social Psychology* 102 no, 3 (2012); Hakan Ozcelik and Sigal Barsade, "Work Loneliness and Employee

Performance," *Academy of Management Annual Meeting Proceedings* (August 1, 2011).

21   For the first mention of this phenomenon, see Anthony Rieber, "Why Yankees Have a Higher Winning Percentage During HOPE Week," *Newsday*, May 27, 2017. The statistics presented herein replicate Rieber's analysis for a slightly newer decade: from 2009 to 2018.

22   Daniel Hedblom, Brent Hickman and John A. List, "Toward an Understanding of Corporate Social Responsibility: Theory and Field Experimental Evidence," National Bureau of Economic Research Working Paper No. 26222, September 2019.

23   Dana Chandlera and Adam Kapelnerb, "Breaking Monotony with Meaning: Motivation in Crowdsourcing Markets," *Journal of Economic Behavior & Organization* 90 (2013).

24   José M. Peiró, Malgorzata Kożusznik and Aida Soriano, "From Happiness Orientations to Work Performance: The Mediating Role of Hedonic and Eudaimonic Experiences," *International Journal of Environmental Research and Public Health* 16, no. 24 (2019).

25   Bea Boccalandro, "Increasing Employee Engagement Through Corporate Volunteering," Voluntare, 2018.

26   Happiness Research Institute and Krifa, "Job Satisfaction Index 2017," Happiness Research Institute, 2017.

27   Joseph Chancellor, Seth Margolis, Katherine Jacobs Bao and Sonya Lyubomirsky, "Everyday Prosociality in the Workplace: The Reinforcing Benefits of Giving, Getting and Glimpsing," *Emotion* 18, no. 4 (2018).

28   Blake A. Allan, Cassondra Batz-Barbarich, Haley M. Sterling and Louis Tay, "Outcomes of Meaningful Work: A Meta-Analysis," *Journal of Management Studies* 56, no.3 (November 12, 2018).

29   Merriam-Webster, Merriam-Webster website, accessed on May 22, 2020.

30   Tristen K. Inagaki, et al., "The Neurobiology of Giving Versus Receiving Support: The Role of Stress-Related and Social Reward-Related Neural Activity, *Psychosomatic Medicine* 78, no. 4 (May 2016).

31   Patrick L. Hill, et al., "Sense of Purpose Moderates the Associations Between Daily Stressors and Daily Well-being," *Annals of Behavioral Medicine* 52, no. 8 (August 2018); Elizabeth B. Raposa, Holly B. Laws and Emily B. Ansell, "Prosocial Behavior Mitigates the Negative Effects of Stress in Everyday Life," *Clinical Psychological Science* 4, no. 4 (December 2015); Jina Park and Roy F. Baumeister, "Meaning in Life and Adjustment to Daily Stressors," *The Journal of Positive Psychology* 12, no. 4 (2017); Michael Poulin and Alison Holman, "Helping Hands, Healthy Body? Oxytocin Receptor Gene and Prosocial Behavior Interact to Buffer the Association Between Stress and Physical Health," *Hormones and Behavior* 63, no. 3 (January 2013).

32   William T. Hallam, et al., "Association Between Adolescent Eudaimonic Behaviours and Emotional Competence in Young Adulthood," *Journal of Happiness Studies* 15, no. 5 (October 2014).

33   Binrian D. Ostafin and Nils Feyel, "The Effects of a Brief Meaning in Life Intervention on the Incentive Salience of Alcohol," *Addictive Behaviors* 90 (March 2019); Joseph Chancellor, Seth Margolis, Katherine Jacobs Bao and Sonya Lyubomirsky, "Everyday Prosociality in the Workplace: The Reinforcing Benefits of Giving, Getting and Glimpsing," *Emotion* 18, no. 4 (2018); Daye Son and Laura M. Padilla-Walker, "Happy Helpers: A Multidimensional and Mixed-

Method Approach to Prosocial Behavior and its Effects on Friendship Quality, Mental Health and Well-being During Adolescence," *Journal of Happiness Studies* (July 2019); Adam M. Grant and Sabine Sonnentag, "Doing Good Buffers Against Feeling Bad: Prosocial Impact Compensates for Negative Task and Self-Evaluations," *Organizational Behavior and Human Decision Processes* 111 (2010); Daniel Shek, "Meaning in Life and Psychological Well-Being: An Empirical Study Using the Chinese Version of the Purpose in Life Questionnaire," *The Journal of Genetic Psychology* 153, no. 2 (July 1992); Stephanie L. Brown, R. Michael Brown, James S. House and Dylan M. Smith, "Coping with Spousal Loss: Potential Buffering Effects of Self-Reported Helping Behavior," *Personality & Social Psychology Bulletin* 34, no. 6 (June 2008); Nadav Klein, "Prosocial Behavior Increases Perceptions of Meaning in Life," *The Journal of Positive Psychology* 12, no. 4 (July 2016); Nicole D. Anderson, et al., "The Benefits Associated With Volunteering Among Seniors: A Critical Review and Recommendations for Future Research," *Psychological Bulletin* 140, no. 6 (August 2014).

34   Shigehiro Oishi and Ed Diener, "Residents of Poor Nations Have a Greater Sense of Meaning in Life Than Residents of Wealthy Nations," *Psychological Science* 25, no. 2 (2014).

35   Victor E. Frankl, *Man's Search for Meaning* (Boston: Beacon Press, 2006).

36   Ashley V. Whillans, Elizabeth W. Dunn, Gillian M. Sandstrom, Sally S. Dickerson and Kenneth M. Madden, "Is Spending Money on Others Good for Your Heart?," *Health Psychology* 35, no. 6 (2016).

37   Hannah M. C. Schreier, Kimberly A. Schonert-Reichl and Edith Chen, "Effect of Volunteering on Risk Factors for Cardiovascular Disease in Adolescents: A Randomized Controlled Trial," *JAMA*

Pediatrics 167, no. 4 (April 2013). See also Eric S. Kim, Scott W. Delaney and Laura D. Kubzansky, "Sense of Purpose in Life and Cardiovascular Disease: Underlying Mechanisms and Future Directions," *Current Cardiology Reports* 21, no. 11 (October 2019).

38   Michael Poulin and Alison Holman, "Helping Hands, Healthy Body? Oxytocin Receptor Gene and Prosocial Behavior Interact to Buffer the Association Between Stress and Physical Health," *Hormones and Behavior* 63, no. 3 (January 2013); Barbara L. Fredrickson, et al., "A Functional Genomic Perspective on Human Well-being, *Proceedings of the National Academy of Sciences* 110, no. 33 (July 2013); Hannah M. C. Schreier, Kimberly A. Schonert-Reichl and Edith Chen, "Effect of Volunteering on Risk Factors for Cardiovascular Disease in Adolescents: A Randomized Controlled Trial," *JAMA Pediatrics* 167, no. 4 (April 2013).

39   Yilu Wang, Jianqiao Ge, Hanqi Zhang, Haixia Wang and Xiaofei Xie, "Altruistic Behaviors Relieve Physical Pain," *Proceedings of the National Academy of Sciences* 117, no. 2 (January 2020).

40   Yilu Wang, Jianqiao Ge, Hanqi Zhang, Haixia Wang and Xiaofei Xie, "Altruistic Behaviors Relieve Physical Pain," *Proceedings of the National Academy of Sciences* 117, no. 2 (January 2020).

41   A. James O'Malley, Samuel Arbesman, Darby Miller Steiger, James H. Fowler and Nicholas A. Christakis, "Egocentric Social Network Structure, Health and Pro-Social Behaviors in a National Panel Study of Americans," *PloS One* 7, no. 5 (May 2012); Astrid M. G. Poorthuis, et al., "Prosocial Tendencies Predict Friendship Quality, But Not for Popular Children," *Journal of Experimental Child Psychology* 112, no. 4 (August 2012); Tess Kay and Steven Bradbury, "Youth Sport Volunteering: Developing Social Capital?," *Sport, Education and*

Society 14, no. 1 (2009); Charlie L. Hardy and Mark Van Vugt, "Nice Guys Finish First: The Competitive Altruism Hypothesis," *Personality and Social Psychology Bulletin* 32 (2006); Robb Willer, "Groups Reward Individual Sacrifice: The Status Solution to the Collective Action Problem," *American Sociological Review* 74 (2009); Ashley Harrell, "Competition for Leadership Promotes Contributions to Collective Action," *Social Forces* 97, no. 1 (September 2018); Ashley Harrell and Brent Simpson, "The Dynamics of Prosocial Leadership: Power and Influence in Collective Action Groups," *Social Forces* 94 (2016); Jacki Fitzpatrick and Donna L. Sollie, "Influence of Individual and Interpersonal Factors on Satisfaction and Stability in Romantic Relationships," *Personal Relationships* 6, no. 3 (May 2005); Elizabeth W. Dunn, Daniel T. Gilbert and Timothy D. Wilson, "If Money Doesn't Make You Happy, Then You Probably Aren't Spending It Right," *Journal of Consumer Psychology* 21, no. 2 (2011); Daye Son and Laura M. Padilla-Walker, "Happy Helpers: A Multidimensional and Mixed-Method Approach to Prosocial Behavior and Its Effects on Friendship Quality, Mental Health and Well-being During Adolescence," *Journal of Happiness Studies* (July 2019).

42   Jorge Moll, Frank Krueger, Roland Zahn, Matteo Pardini, Ricardo de Oliveira-Souza and Jordan Grafman, "Human Front-Mesolimbic Networks Guide Decisions About Charitable Donation," *Proceedings of the National Academy of Sciences* 103, no. 42 (October 2006); Soyoung Q. Park, Thorsten Kahnt, Azade Dogan, Sabrina Strang, Ernst Fehr and Philippe N. Tobler, "A Neural Link Between Generosity and Happiness." *Nature Communications* 8, 15964 (2017).

43   Lara B. Aknin, et al., "Prosocial Spending and Well-Being: Cross-Cultural Evidence for a Psychological Universal," *Journal*

of Personality and Social Psychology 104, no. 4 (2013); Lara B. Aknin, Ashley V. Whillans, Michael I. Norton and Elizabeth W. Dunn, "Happiness and Prosocial Behavior: An Evaluation of the Evidence," World Happiness Report 2019, United Nations Sustainable Development Solutions Network (2019); Lee Rowland & Oliver Scott Curry, "A Range of Kindness Activities Boost Happiness," *The Journal of Social Psychology* 159, no. 3 (2019); Christopher P. Niemiec, Richard M. Ryan and Edward L. Deci, "Consequences of Attaining Intrinsic and Extrinsic Aspirations in Post-College Life," *Journal of Research in Personality* 73, no. 3 (2009); Evelien Snippe, Bertus F. Jeronimus, Marije aan het Rot, Elisabeth H. Bos, Peter de Jonge and Marieke Wichers, "The Reciprocity of Prosocial Behavior and Positive Affect in Daily Life," *Journal of Personality* 86, no. 2 (January 2017).

44 Daye Son and Laura M. Padilla-Walker, "Happy Helpers: A Multidimensional and Mixed-Method Approach to Prosocial Behavior and Its Effects on Friendship Quality, Mental Health and Well-being During Adolescence," *Journal of Happiness Studies* (July 2019).

45 Sabine Sonnentag and Adam M. Grant, "Doing Good at Work Feels Good at Home, But Not Right Away: When and Why Perceived Prosocial Impact Predicts Positive Affect," *Personnel Psychology* 65, no. 3 (September 2012).

46 S. Katherine Nelson, Kristin Layous, Steven W. Cole and Sonja Lyubomirsky, "Do Unto Others or Treat Yourself? The Effects of Prosocial and Self-Focused Behavior on Psychological Flourishing," *Emotion* 16, no. 6 (2016), p. 859.

47 Joseph Chancellor, Seth Margolis, Katherine Jacobs Bao and Sonya Lyubomirsky, "Everyday Prosociality in the Workplace: The Reinforcing Benefits of Giving, Getting and Glimpsing,"

Emotion 18, no. 4 (2018); Lara B. Aknin, et al., "Prosocial Spending and Well-Being: Cross-Cultural Evidence for a Psychological Universal," *Journal of Personality and Social Psychology* 104, no. 4 (2013).

48   Lara B. Aknin, Alice L. Fleerackers and Kiley J. Hamlin, "Can Third-Party Observers Detect the Emotional Rewards of Generous Spending?," *The Journal of Positive Psychology* 9, no. 3 (2014); S. Katherine Nelson, Kristin Layous, Steven W. Cole and Sonja Lyubomirsky, "Do Unto Others or Treat Yourself? The Effects of Prosocial and Self-Focused Behavior on Psychological Flourishing," *Emotion* 16, no. 6 (2016). See also Joseph Chancellor, Seth Margolis, Katherine Jacobs Bao and Sonya Lyubomirsky, "Everyday Prosociality in the Workplace: The Reinforcing Benefits of Giving, Getting and Glimpsing," *Emotion* 18, no. 4 (2018); Katherine Nelson, Matthew D. Della Porta, Katherine Jacobs Bao, HyunJung Crystal Lee, Incheol Choi and Sonja Lyubomirsky, "'It's Up to You': Experimentally Manipulated Autonomy Support for Prosocial Behavior Improves Well-Being in Two Cultures Over Six Weeks," *The Journal of Positive Psychology* 10, no. 5 (2015).

49   Morris Alan Okun, Ellen W. Yeung and Stephanie Willen Brown, "Volunteering by Older Adults and Risk of Mortality: A Meta-Analysis," *Psychology and Aging* 28, no. 2 (February 2013). See also Michael Poulin, Stephanie L. Brown, Amanda Dillard and Dylan M. Smith, "Giving to Others and the Association Between Stress and Mortality," *American Journal of Public Health* 103, no. 9 (2013), and Randy Cohen, Craig Bavishi and Alan Rozanski, "Purpose in Life and Its Relationship to All-Cause Mortality and Cardiovascular Events: A Meta-Analysis," *Psychosomatic Medicine* 78, no. 2 (2015).

50 Andrew Reece, Gabriella Kellerman and Alexi Robichaux, "Meaning and Purpose at Work," BetterUp, 2018.

51 Shawn Achor, "The Value of Happiness," *Harvard Business Review* (January 2012).

52 Mara Gordon, "What's Your Purpose? Finding A Sense of Meaning In Life Is Linked To Health," Health Shots NPR, May 25, 2019.

53 Richard M. Piech, et al., "People with Higher Interoceptive Sensitivity are More Altruistic, But Improving Interoception Does Not Increase Altruism," *Scientific Reports* 7, no. 15652 (November 2017).

54 EarthShare, "The New Business Imperative: Employees Turn Environmental Action into a Workplace Necessity," EarthShare, 2019.

55 John B. Izzo and Jeff Vanderwielen, *The Purpose Revolution: How Leaders Create Engagement and Competitive Advantage in an Age of Social Good* (Oakland: Berrett-Koehler Publishers, 2018).

56 Nate Dvorak, "Three Ways Mission-Driven Workplaces Perform Better," Gallup website, April 4, 2017, accessed on May 22, 2020; William Phanuel Kofi Darbi, "Of Mission and Vision Statements and Their Potential Impact on Employee Behaviour and Attitudes: The Case of a Public But Profit-Oriented Tertiary Institution," *International Journal of Business and Social Science* 3, no. 14 (Special Issue-July 2012).

57 Andrew Reece, Gabriella Kellerman and Alexi Robichaux, "Meaning and Purpose at Work," BetterUp (2018); The Energy Project, "The Human Era @ Work: Findings from The Energy Project and *Harvard Business Review* 2014" (New York: The Energy Project, 2014).

58 The concept of job purposing builds on the concept of "job crafting" that Amy Wrzesniewski and Jane Dutton introduced

in 2001. Job crafting involves workers shaping their own work environment to fit their individual needs. It includes adjusting responsibilities, relationships and almost any part of the job. By focusing only on adjusting the social purpose a job has, job purposing can be considered a subset of job crafting.

59   Steve Fiorillo, "What Is Oprah Winfrey's Net Worth?" The Street website, May 31, 2019, accessed on August 23, 2019.

60   Oprah Winfrey, "Dream Big," *O Magazine* 3 no. 9 (September 2002).

61   Studs Terkel, *Working: People Talk About What They Do All Day and How They Feel About What They Do* (New York: The New Press, 1997).

62   Joseph Chancellor, Seth Margolis, Katherine Jacobs Bao and Sonya Lyubomirsky, "Everyday Prosociality in the Workplace: The Reinforcing Benefits of Giving, Getting and Glimpsing," *Emotion* 18, no. 4 (2018).

63   Catherine Bailey and Adrian Madden, "Time Reclaimed: Temporality and the Experience of Meaningful Work," *Work, Employment and Society* 31, no. 1 (Feb 2017).

64   Morten T. Hansen, *Great at Work: How Top Performers Do Less, Work Better and Achieve More* (New York: Simon & Schuster, 2018).

65   Morten T. Hansen, *Find Success in Your Career by Learning How to Match Your Passion With Your Purpose*, Morten Hansen website, April 27, 2019, accessed on May 28, 2019.

66   Jeff Joireman, Dustin Smith, Richie Liu and Jonathan Arthurs, "It's All Good: Corporate Social Responsibility Promotes Positive Response to Service Failures Among Value Aligned Customers," *Journal of Public Policy & Marketing* 34, no. 1 (April 1, 2015).

67   Joan C. Williams and Sky Mihaylo, "How the Best Bosses
      Interrupt Bias on Their Teams," *Harvard Business Review*
      (November-December 2019).

68   Interface, *The Interface Story*, Interface website, accessed on
      January 3, 2020.

69   Cornelia Dean, "Executive on a Mission: Saving the Planet,"
      New York Times, May 22, 2007; Interface, *Interface Announces
      Mission Zero Success, Commits to Climate Take Back*, Cision PR
      Newswire website, November 4, 2019, accessed on December 1,
      2019.

70   Daniel J. Simons and Christopher F. Chabris, "Gorillas in Our
      Midst: Sustained Inattentional Blindness for Dynamic Events,"
      Perception 28, no. 9 (1999).

71   Andrew Reece, Gabriella Kellerman and Alexi Robichaux,
      "Meaning and Purpose at Work," BetterUp, 2018; Nathan P.
      Podsakoff, Steven W. Whiting, Philip M. Podsakoff and Brian
      D. Blume, "Individual- and Organizational-Level Consequences
      of Organizational Citizenship Behaviors: A Meta-Analysis,"
      Journal of Applied Psychology, 94 (2009); Shawn Achor, "The
      Value of Happiness," *Harvard Business Review* (January 2012).

72   Sara Konrath, Andrea Fuhrel-Forbis, Alina Lou and Stephanie
      Brown, "Motives for Volunteering Are Associated With
      Mortality Risk in Older Adults," *Health Psychology* 31, no. 1
      (January 2012).

73   Christina Maslach, Wilmar B. Schaufeli and Michael P. Leiter,
      "Job Burnout," *Annual Review of Psychology* 52 (2001).

74   Barbara Lombardo and Caryl Eyre, "Compassion Fatigue: A
      Nurse's Primer," *Online Journal of Issues in Nursing* 16, no. 1
      (2011).

75   Olga Klimecki and Tania Singer, "Empathic Distress Fatigue
      Rather than Compassion Fatigue? Integrating Findings from

Empathy Research in Psychology and Neuroscience," in *Pathological Altruism,* eds: Barbara Ann Oakley, Ariel Knafo, Michal Guruprasad Madhavan and David Sloan Wilson (New York: Springer, 2012); Matthieu Ricard, *Altruism: The Power of Compassion to Change Yourself and the World* (New York: Little, Brown and Company, 2015).

76   Carol Horowitz, Anthony L. Suchman, William T. Branch and Richard M. Frankel, "What Do Doctors Find Meaningful About Their Work?," *Annals of Internal Medicine* 138, no.9 (2003).

77   Frank Marela and Richard M. Ryan, "Prosocial Behavior Increases Well-Being and Vitality Even Without Contact With the Beneficiary: Causal and Behavioral Evidence," *Motivation and Emotion* 40, no. 3 (June 2016).

78   Adam M. Grant and Sabine Sonnentag, "Doing Good Buffers Against Feeling Bad: Prosocial Impact Compensates for Negative Task and Self-Evaluations," *Organizational Behavior and Human Decision Processes* 111 (2010).

79   Dermot O'Reilly, Sheelah Connolly, Michael Rosato and Chris Patterson, "Is Caring Associated with an Increased Risk of Mortality? A Longitudinal Study," *Social Science & Medicine* 67, no. 8 (October 2008).

80   Melinda Gates, *The Moment of Lift: How Empowering Women Changes the World* (New York: Flatiron Books, 2019).

81   Bill Gates and Melinda Gates, "Text of the 2014 Commencement address by Bill & Melinda Gates," Stanford News website, accessed on May 14, 2019.

82   Sonja Lyubomirsky, "Hedonic Adaptation to Positive and Negative Experiences," *The Oxford Handbook of Stress, Health, and Coping* by Susan Folkman (Ed.), (Oxford University Press, 2011).

83   Eva H. Telzer, Andrew J. Fuligni, Matthew D. Lieberman
      and Adriana Galván, "Neural Sensitivity to Eudaimonic and
      Hedonic Rewards Differentially Predict Adolescent Depressive
      Symptoms Over Time," *Proceedings of the National Academy of
      Sciences* 111, no. 18 (April 2014).

84   Filip Lievens, Deniz S. Ones and Stephan Dilchert, "Personality
      Scale Validities Increase Throughout Medical School," *The
      Journal of Applied Psychology* 94, no. 6 (November 2009).

85   Carsten K.W. De Dreu and Aukje Nauta, "Self-interest and
      Other-orientation in Organizational Behavior: Implications for
      Job Performance, Prosocial Behavior, and Personal Initiative,"
      Journal of Applied Psychology, 94, no. 4 (2009).

86   Adam M. Grant, *Give and Take: Why Helping Others Drives Our
      Success* (New York: Penguin Books, 2013).

87   Jeremy A. Frimer, et al., "The Integration of Agency and
      Communion in Moral Personality: Evidence of Enlightened
      Self-Interest," *Journal of Personality and Social Psychology* 101, no.
      1 (July 2011).

88   Sara B. Algoe and Jonathan Haidt, "Witnessing Excellence in
      Action: The 'Other-Praising' Emotions of Elevation, Gratitude
      and Admiration," *The Journal of Positive Psychology* 4, no. 2
      (February 2009.

89   "Kenneth Cole: On How To Creatively Break Into The Career
      Of Your Choice," On Purpose with Jay Shetty podcast, October
      21, 2019.

90   Work for Good, *The Nonprofit Workforce Speaks: Candid Insight
      to Attract, Engage and Retain Top Mission-Driven Talent,* Work
      for Good Report, 2019.

91   Maxxia, "The Workplace Insights Not-for-Profit Sentiment
      Study," Maxxia Workplace Insights, 2013.

92   Work for Good, *The Nonprofit Workforce Speaks: Candid Insight to Attract, Engage and Retain Top Mission-Driven Talent,* Work for Good Report, 2019.

93   Heather Joslyn, "Nonprofit Employees Are More Satisfied Than Other Workers With Their Jobs, Says New Brookings Survey - But Problems Loom," *The Chronicle of Philanthropy* 10 (October 2002).

94   Lisa Birnbach and Kenneth Cole, *This Is a Kenneth Cole Production,* (New York: Rizzoli International Publications, Inc, 2013).

95   Indeed Editorial Team, *The Top-Rated Workplaces in 2019,* Indeed Blog website, July 16, 2019, accessed on August 9, 2019.

96   Daniel Hedblom, Brent R. Hickman and John A. List, "Toward an Understanding of Corporate Social Responsibility: Theory and Field Experimental Evidence," National Bureau of Economic Research Working Paper no. 26222 (September 2019).

97   Nell Allen, "Nonprofit Talent Management: Using Compensation, Benefits and Incentives to Effectively Attract and Retain Top Talent Employees at Nonprofit Organizations," (Dissertation: University of Maryland University College: ProQuest Publishing, 2018).

98   EarthShare, "The New Business Imperative: Employees Turn Environmental Action into a Workplace Necessity," EarthShare, 2019.

99   Christiane Bode, Jasjit Singh and Michelle Rogan, "Corporate Social Initiatives and Employee Retention," *Organizational Science* (November-December 2015).

100   Vanessa C. Burbano, "Social Responsibility Messages and Worker Wage Requirements: Field Experimental Evidence from

Online Labor Marketplaces," *Organization Science* 27, no. 4 (2016).

101 Andrew Reece, Gabriella Kellerman and Alexi Robichaux, "Meaning and Purpose at Work," BetterUp, 2018.

102 Randall Beck and Jim Harter, "Companies Are Missing Opportunities for Growth and Revenue," *Business Journal* (April 28, 2015).

103 Gallup, *State of the Global Workplace*, Gallup Press, 2017.

104 Bea Boccalandro, "Increasing Employee Engagement Through Corporate Volunteering," Voluntare, 2018.

105 Blake A. Allan, Cassondra Batz-Barbarich, Haley M. Sterling and Louis Tay, "Outcomes of Meaningful Work: A Meta-Analysis," *Journal of Management Studies* 56, no. 3 (November 12, 2018).

106 Jia Hu and Robert Liden, "Making a Difference in the Teamwork: Linking Team Prosocial Motivation to Team Processes and Effectiveness," *Academy of Management Journal* 58, no. 4 (January 2014).

107 Jia Hu and Robert Liden, "Making a Difference in the Teamwork: Linking Team Prosocial Motivation to Team Processes and Effectiveness," *Academy of Management Journal* 58, no. 4 (January 2014).

108 Lalin Anik, Lara B. Aknin, Michael I. Norton, Elizabeth W. Dunn and Jordi Quoidbach, "Prosocial Bonuses Increase Employee Satisfaction and Team Performance," *PLoS ONE* 8, no. 9 (2013); Andrew Reece, Gabriella Kellerman and Alexi Robichaux, "Meaning and Purpose at Work," BetterUp, 2018.

109 Dove, "Dove Self-Esteem Project," Dove website, accessed on May 1, 2020.

110 Diana Marszalek, "For Consumers, Brand Purpose Is Emotional," The Holmes Report: Porter Novelli/Cone Feeling Purpose Study, May 29, 2019.

111 Rachel Barton, Masataka Ishikawa, Kevin Quiring and Bill Theofilou, "From Me to We: The Rise of the Purpose-led Brand," Accenture, 2018.

112 Richard Aldwinckle, "Making Purpose Pay: Inspiring Sustainable Living," Unilever, 2017.

113 Thomas W. Malnight, Ivy Buche and Charles Dhanaraj, "Put Purpose at the Core of Your Strategy," *Harvard Business Review* (September-October 2019).

114 Ashley Harrell, "Competition for Leadership Promotes Contributions to Collective Action," *Social Forces* 97, no. 1 (September 2018); Ashley Harrell and Brent Simpson, "The Dynamics of Prosocial Leadership: Power and Influence in Collective Action Groups," *Social Forces* 94 (2016); Robb Willer, "Groups Reward Individual Sacrifice: The Status Solution to the Collective Action Problem," *American Sociological Review* 74 (2009); Charlie L. Hardy and Mark Van Vugt, "Nice Guys Finish First: The Competitive Altruism Hypothesis," *Personality and Social Psychology Bulletin* 32 (2006).

115 EY, "Purpose-Driven Leadership," EY, 2018.

116 Havas Group, "Meaningful Brands° 2017 Reap Greater Financial Rewards as They Outperform the Stock Market by 206%," Havas Group, February 1, 2017.

117 David C. McClelland and Carol Kirshnit, "The Effect of Motivational Arousal Through Films on Salivary Immunoglobulin A," *Psychology & Health* 2, no. 1 (1988).

118 Ante Glavas, "Corporate Social Responsibility and Employee Engagement: Enabling Employees to Employ More of Their

Whole Selves at Work," *Frontiers in Psychology* 7, no. 796 (May 31, 2016).

119 Michael I. Norton, Daniel Mochon and Dan Ariely, "The IKEA Effect: When Labor Leads to Love," *Journal of Consumer Psychology* 22, no. 3 (July 2012).

120 Dan Ariely, Emir Kamenica and Drazen Prelec, "Man's Search for Meaning: The Case of Legos," *Journal of Economic Behavior & Organization* 67 (2008).

121 Adam Grant, "The Significance of Task Significance: Job Performance Effects, Relational Mechanisms and Boundary Conditions," *Journal of Applied Psychology* 93, no. 1 (2008); Nicola Bellé, "Experimental Evidence on the Relationship Between Public Service Motivation and Job Performance," *Public Administration Review* 73, no. 1 (January 2013); Iris Lok and Elizabeth W. Dunn, "Under What Conditions Does Prosocial Spending Promote Happiness?," *Collabra: Psychology* 6, no. 1 (2020).

122 Jonathan Haidt, *The Happiness Hypothesis: Finding Modern Truth in Ancient Wisdom* (New York: Basic Books, 2006)

123 Adam M. Grant, Elizabeth M. Campbell, Grace Chen, Keenan Cottone, David Lapedis and Karen Lee, "Impact and the Art of Motivation Maintenance: The Effects of Contact With Beneficiaries on Persistence Behavior," *Organizational Behavior and Human Decision Processes* 103, no. 1 (May 2007). See also Adam M. Grant, "The Significance of Task Significance: Job Performance Effects, Relational Mechanisms, and Boundary Conditions," *Journal of Applied Psychology* 93, no. 1 (2008).

124 Paul Green, Francesca Gino and Bradley R. Staats, "Seeking to Belong: How the Words of Internal and External Beneficiaries Influence Performance," Harvard Business School Working Paper 17-073, 2017.

125   Ellen J. Langer, *Mindfulness: 25th Anniversary Edition* (Boston: Da Capo Press, 2014).

126   Ellen J. Langer, *Mindfulness: 25th Anniversary Edition* (Boston: Da Capo Press, 2014).

127   Sabine Sonnentag and Adam M. Grant, "Doing Good at Work Feels Good at Home, But Not Right Away: When and Why Perceived Prosocial Impact Predicts Positive Affect," *Personnel Psychology* 65, no. 3 (September 2012).

128   Bureau of Labor Statistics, "Job Openings and Labor Turnover," Bureau of Labor Statistics (January, 2020).

129   An-Chih Wang, et al., "Benevolence-Dominant, Authoritarianism-Dominant, and Classical Paternalistic Leadership: Testing Their Relationships With Subordinate Performance," *The Leadership Quarterly* 29, no. 6 (December 2018).

130   David Whyte, *Crossing the Unknown Sea: Work as a Pilgrimage of Identity* (New York: Riverhead Books, 2001).

131   Thomas Hobbes, *Leviathan or The Matter, Form, and Power of a Commonwealth Ecclesiastical and Civil* (Pacific Publishing Studio, 2011).

132   Victoria Hornera, Devyn Cartera, Malini Suchaka and Frans B. M. de Waal, "Spontaneous Prosocial Choice by Chimpanzees," *Proceedings of the National Academy of Sciences of the United States of America* 108, no. 33 (August 16, 2011).

133   Martin Schmelza, et al., "Chimpanzees Return Favors at a Personal Cost," *Proceedings of the National Academy of Sciences of the United States of America* 114, no. 28 (July 11, 2017).

134   Felix Warneken et al., "Spontaneous Altruism by Chimpanzees and Young Children," *PLoS Biology* 5, no. 7 (2007).

135 Jules H. Masserman, Stanley Wechkin and William Terris, "Altruistic Behavior in Rhesus Monkeys," *The American Journal of Psychiatry* 121 (December 1964).

136 American Psychiatric Association, *Diagnostic and Statistical Manual of Mental Disorders, Fifth Edition DSM-5* (Arlington: American Psychiatric Publishing, 2013).

137 Roman Krznaric, *Empathy: Why It Matters, and How to Get It* (New York: Perigree, 2014).

138 Alexandra G. Rosati, Lauren M. DiNicola and Joshua W. Buckholtz, "Chimpanzee Cooperation is Fast and Independent from Self-Control," *Psychological Science* 29, no. 11 (October 8, 2018).

139 Shalom H. Schwartz, "An Overview of the Schwartz Theory of Basic Values," *Online Readings in Psychology and Culture* 2, no. 1 (2012).

140 Peter Gray, "Play as the Foundation for Hunter-Gatherer Social Existence," *American Journal of Play* 1, no. 4 (2009).

141 Peter Gray, "Play Makes Us Human V: Why Hunter-Gatherers' Work is Play," Psychology Today blog, July 2, 2009, accessed on August 4, 2019.

142 Irina Komarovskaya, et al., "The Impact of Killing and Injuring Others on Mental Health Symptoms Among Police Officers," *Journal of Psychiatric Research* 45, no. 10 (October 2011).

143 Richard Wrangham, *The Goodness Paradox: The Strange Relationship Between Virtue and Violence in Human Evolution* (New York: Vintage, 2019); Christopher Boehm, "Retaliatory Violence in Human Prehistory," *The British Journal of Criminology*, Volume 51, no 3, May 2011.

144 Heather Whipps, "Peace or War? How Early Humans Behaved," Live Science website, March 16, 2006, accessed on August 4, 2019.

145 "What Happens When You Give Someone a Chance to Be Honest?" Honest Tea website, accessed on December 31, 2018.

146 Alain Cohn, Michel André Maréchal, David Tannenbaum and Christian Lukas Zünd, "Civic Honesty Around the Globe," *Science* 365, no. 6448 (July 2019).

147 John M. Darley and C. Daniel Batson, "From Jerusalem to Jericho: A Study of Situational and Dispositional Variables in Helping Behavior," *Journal of Personality and Social Psychology* 27, no. 1 (1973).

148 Richard Donkin, *The History of Work* (Basingstoke, United Kingdom: Palgrave Macmillan, 2010).

149 U.S. Bureau of Labor Statistics, "American Time Use Survey, 2019," U.S. Bureau of Labor Statistics website, accessed on February 2, 2020.

150 Highway and Transportation District Authority, "Golden Gate Bridge," Highway and Transportation District Authority website, accessed on January 26, 2020.

151 Joseph Chancellor, Seth Margolis, Katherine Jacobs Bao and Sonya Lyubomirsky, "Everyday Prosociality in the Workplace: The Reinforcing Benefits of Giving, Getting, and Glimpsing," *Emotion* 18, no. 4 (2018).

152 Barry Feinberg and Ronald Kasrils, editors, *Bertrand Russell's America: 1896-1945* (New York: Viking Press, 1974).

153 Will Dahlgren, "Chinese People Are Most Likely to Feel the World is Getting Better," YouGov website, January 5, 2016, accessed on March 28, 2020.

154 Max Roser, Esteban Ortiz-Ospina and Hannah Ritchie, "Life Expectancy," Our World in Data website, October 2019, accessed on March 28, 2020.

155 Our World in Data website, accessed on March 28, 2020; United Nations, "The Millennium Development Goals Report 2015," United Nations, 2015.

156 U.S. Bureau of Economic Analysis, "Gross Domestic Product by Industry and Input-Output Statistics," April, 2019; U.S. Internal Revenue Service, "Receipts by Source: 1924 - 2024," Washington: Government Publishing Office; Giving USA, "Giving USA 2019: The Annual Report on Philanthropy for the Year 2018," Giving USA, June 18, 2019.

157 Steven Pinker, *Enlightenment Now: The Case for Reason, Science, Humanism, and Progress* (New York: Penguin Books, 2018).

158 Bill & Melinda Gates Foundation, "Annual Report 2018," Bill & Melinda Gates Foundation, 2019.

Printed in the USA
CPSIA information can be obtained
at www.ICGtesting.com
JSHW022331140824
68134JS00019B/1419